MW00668251

Rachel Sherburne shares her jou
hope can be found: in a relationsᵢᵤₚ
Holy Spirit. Through her experience growing up in a military family,
later as an Air Force officer serving in war-torn Iraq, through a relationship that didn't happen, to one that did but ended in brokenness, Rachel
reveals a broader perspective about hope, what truly makes us happy,
and how life is ultimately about loving God, loving others, and loving
one's self. Once I started reading her book, I couldn't put it down.
Everyone can learn from Rachel's story. Thanks for your vulnerability,
Rachel.

—Diane Paddison
Founder of 4word and author of *Work, Love, Pray*
Former C-Suite Executive in two Fortune 500 companies
Wife and mother of four

Reading *Unbounded Hope* was like having deep conversations with a
good friend. Rachel poured her heart out on each page, sharing issues
in her life that ring true in all of our lives. We all struggle! She offers up
what she's learned in those struggles along with biblical truths and tangible takeaways that inspire hope in Christ and will encourage authentic
community and conversation.

—Jackie Mosley
Sr. Publisher, RightNow Media

A jewel… This book is full of wisdom that could only be God-inspired;
Rachel is wise beyond her years. Life happens – Kudos to Rachel for
practical steps on how to choose hope and healing over depression and
despair.

—Erin Botsford
CEO of The Botsford Group
Best-selling author of *The Big Retirement Risk*

UNBOUNDED
HOPE

Releasing What You Think You Want and

Gaining Everything You Truly Need

RACHEL SHERBURNE

HIGH BRIDGE BOOKS

HOUSTON

High Bridge Books titles may be purchased in bulk for educational, business, fundraising, or sales promotional use. For information please contact High Bridge Books via www.HighBridgeBooks.com/contact.

Published in Houston, Texas by High Bridge Books

DEDICATED TO…

God, the eternal and unbounded source of all hope.

My amazing family and friends who have loved me so well on this journey.

Everyone who is searching for hope. May this book encourage and guide you on your way.

To carol,
keep choosing hope!
♡
Rachel Shubin

CONTENTS

SEARCHING FOR HOPE

Once you choose hope, anything is possible.

—CHRISTOPHER REEVE

Hope changes everything. It's what fuels us to get out of bed in the morning, chase our dreams, overcome obstacles, and believe that we can truly live an incredible life despite what anybody else says.

Since my days as a young girl, I've always wanted the "fairytale." You know… beauty, success, significance, an incredible romance, and then wedded bliss. I believed having these things would make all my dreams come true. But somehow, I glossed over the fact that fairytales always contain some sort of evil or tragedy. I thought the happy ending was a guarantee and the painful part was optional. I know now that it's not.

Every life is a beautiful story with at least one tragedy or significant trial. It could be the loss of a job or a loved one, an illness, a financial crisis, a broken relationship, or something else entirely. But I'm convinced that, at some point, we'll all face something that will shake us to the core and cause us great pain.

A few years ago, I faced an unexpected personal trial. I'd lost loved ones, experienced failure, and endured a broken heart before. But when my marriage of 14 months was rocked with infidelity and my husband moved out, I felt as if my whole world had been turned upside down. Our relationship was a wreck, my self-confidence and sense of security had been decimated, and I didn't know what to do. Everything I had previously hoped in could not get me through the storm I was facing. There was no romance or wedded bliss. What I looked like on the outside couldn't alleviate my heartache. And no amount of success at work or significance in the eyes of others could distract me from the reality of my situation.

The flaw in my hope strategy became blatantly obvious. If hope was based on having all these things, I was out of luck. And then, what about the people who aren't beautiful in the world's eyes? Those who are single? Divorced? Out of a job? Or simply living with unfavorable circumstances beyond their control? Where was the hope for them?

Needing a new strategy, I started researching, reading books, and talking to people who could possibly offer some insight about hope and help me find it. But while everyone agreed it was a marvelous thing and that the best lives were full of it, nobody could offer me tangible steps to lead me from despair to hope; that's what I needed more than anything else!

So, I began praying fervently, vowing to God that, if He would unveil this pathway, I would share it with others. Over the next two years, He answered my prayer by teaching me how to let go, be open to change, walk by faith, forgive, and learn to love. These five principles seemed simple at first, but I soon discovered that living them out would require humility, surrender, trust, and a lot of God's grace. Still, I committed to mastering each one, and despite my own shortcomings and mistakes, the results were remarkable.

True to my promise to God, this book is my story of my life-long search and discovery of the hope that not only helped me to endure my life's toughest challenge so far but also to thrive and become better because of it.

But my search didn't begin in the midst of my broken marriage. It started when I was a young girl desperate for beauty and then as a teenager trying to attain success in life. My journey continued as a young woman looking for significance and searching for an incredible romance. And it climaxed as a new wife hoping for wedded bliss, only to find myself experiencing nothing of the sort.

Throughout this book, I share my struggles, victories, tough choices, and deepest fears and insecurities... the ones I believe most of us have faced but few are willing to talk about. I recount how I learned to love myself and others, overcome obstacles, and pursue my dreams. I share how God has changed my perspective and led me to a place of real, unbounded hope in every area of my life.

To help you discover this unbounded hope for yourself, I have provided personal reflection and/or group discussion questions at the end of each chapter and "Tangible Takeaways" at the end of each section.

If you're facing a tragedy, dealing with challenging circumstances, or your life just hasn't turned out the way you thought it would, I know how tempting it is at times to lay down your hopes and dreams and assume things will never be good again... much less great. I've felt that way, too, and I've been there. But I've learned you don't have to stay there.

It is my genuine desire that this book will challenge your expectations, give you a renewed perspective, minimize unnecessary suffering, and inspire and encourage you along your own journey to hope that knows no limits. When you inevitably find yourself in the storms of life, your response won't be limited to fear, anger, depression, or despair. By letting go, being open to change, walking by faith, forgiving, and learning to love, you can discover real, lasting, and unbounded hope. This kind of hope isn't dependent on your age, looks, job title, bank account, circumstances, or relationship status. It can never be taken from you. And it truly does change *everything* for the better.

It's time to take the limits off of your expectations and embrace unbounded hope.

Part 1

HOPING IN BEAUTY

1

THE QUEST FOR BEAUTY

I noticed a young girl about five years old playing on the beach recently. She laughed loudly and skipped around in the sand as the wind played with her hair, sending it in a thousand different directions. She ran around with freedom and a zeal for life that was more than inspiring. It was beautiful. *She* was beautiful. Her hair was a mess. There wasn't an ounce of makeup on her cute but rather plain face, and her little girlish body was far from the world's definition of sexy. But as I studied her, I was temporarily mesmerized. There was this light in her eyes that revealed the unbroken spirit of a girl who was completely authentic and comfortable being herself without trying to be anything different.

As I watched her, I felt joy and sadness at the same time. *Joy* in recognizing true beauty at its very essence. *Sadness* in realizing how long it had been since I felt like that little girl.

By third grade, I knew what the world defined as beautiful based on what I saw on television, the adult conversations I overheard, and what my classmates were saying. It seemed that beauty was the key to being successful, popular, and pursued by the opposite sex. And because I wanted all of that, I naturally concluded that outer beauty mattered most and that I needed it.

At nine years old, I remember standing in front of my full-length mirror in a swimsuit and assessing my reflection: legs, too thick and muscular; waist, not narrow or flat enough; skin, too pale; and face, not very pretty. Already a harsh critic, it didn't help when, the following year, a boy in my class made fun of the bump on my nose, calling it a "bird beak." My classmates laughed while I adamantly insisted I had no such thing. Up until that point, I had never seen my profile. But when I went home and inspected it in the bathroom mirror, my heart sank. There was a slight bump on my nose. Now, I had something else to feel insecure about.

My mom wouldn't allow me to wear makeup until I was in junior high, but that didn't stop me from secretly experimenting with hers. Just like I'd seen her do hundreds of times, I'd carefully apply her eyeshadow, blush, and lipstick and admire my reflection in the mirror. Because I would always wash my face before she saw me, she didn't have a clue—that is, until the day I tried my hand at her tweezers. Plucking the stray hairs between my eyebrows proved much too tedious, and that's when I got a brilliant idea simply to shave them off. Taking her razor, I did one, painless swipe between my eyes; just like that, they were gone.

Unfortunately, I didn't stop there. After three more swipes, a uni-brow was no longer a problem. The newly exposed skin had never seen the light of day and further highlighted the fact that I had effectively shaved off about half of my eyebrows. I hoped my mom wouldn't notice, but the moment she saw me, she shrieked and said, "Oh, my God! What did you do to yourself?!" Needless to say, it was the first and last time I ever took a razor to my face.

While I wouldn't have described myself as beautiful, I never considered myself unattractive until the day a group of mean girls called me "flat-out ugly" during recess at school. I pretended like I didn't care, but the anger, hurt, and embarrassment built up all day and spilled over into tears when I got home. Sobbing to my mom, I told her what happened and that my only hope of ever being attractive was for me to get braces, a nose job, and a tan. She hugged me, told me I was beautiful, and assured me that these girls were just jealous of me. But her words couldn't heal my wounded ego or change my resolve. I'd fix my teeth, nose, and skin to show those girls I was far from ugly.

Two years later, I got braces. When they came off 18 months later, I couldn't stop smiling. Not only were my teeth straight, but

I had officially checked the first item off my three-phased beauty improvement plan. From that point on, I set my sights on fixing my nose. I'd been teased about the bump on it for years and had tried everything from bangs to convincing my parents I needed glasses in an attempt to minimize it. With 20/20 vision, that didn't work. But I was eagerly awaiting the day when I would be old enough to be a candidate for a rhinoplasty.

Three weeks before I turned 16, my dream came true. It was technically medical surgery covered by insurance to repair my deviated septum, but for an additional fee of $600, the doctor was willing to do a little bit of cosmetic work to reduce the appearance of the bump on top. My parents agreed on one condition: I had to pay for half of it. Ecstatic, I happily handed over all the babysitting money I had saved up and worked out a payment plan with them to cover the rest.

My excitement was tempered when I woke up in the recovery room after surgery throwing up and feeling like I had been punched in the face. After a few days, I was doing better, certain that my new-and-improved nose was beneath the bandage and all the bruising and swelling. Two weeks later, the doctor removed it and gave me a mirror to inspect my profile. In reality, it didn't look all that different, but because the bump was slightly less noticeable, my self-confidence instantly soared. With straight teeth and a new nose, I focused on the third and final thing I needed to improve upon: my fair skin.

I remember my mom telling people about the difference between my sister's coloring and mine. She had skin the color of coffee mixed with cream. My skin was just cream. And I hated it. Sure that a tan would make me more attractive, I applied some of my sister's darker foundation all over my face to test my theory. My eyes seemed greener, my teeth looked whiter, and my full, red lips were not as stark. That sealed the deal. I needed a tan. Period.

Because of my parent's concern about skin cancer, sunbathing and tanning beds were out of the question. So, I began experimenting with the newest and hottest cosmetic products on the market at the time: self-tanners. Regardless of the brand and how well I tried to apply it, I always ended up with a streaked complexion; orange hands, knees, and elbows; and an unpleasant odor that I could never shower off. If those side effects weren't clues that my tan came from a bottle, in three to five days when it started to wear off unevenly, I would be left with a myriad of skin tones. I ended up looking and smelling more like a science project gone wrong than a bronzed beauty. But none of this stopped me.

Just when I was starting to feel better about my appearance, it began to change thanks to puberty. Unlike the girls who developed curves in all the right places, I just gained weight all over and got pimples. My "love relationship" with my body was already strained, but the day I noticed a tiny bit of cellulite on the backs of my thighs, it was over.

I decided to try a diet and hoped Slim Fast would be the solution. My intention was to drink only one can at school, but between playing sports and my high metabolism, I would get so hungry that it was usually gone by mid-morning. By the time I walked into the cafeteria famished a few hours later, my diet was usually sabotaged by chicken nuggets, pizza, or french fries. Considering that Slim Fast is intended to be a meal replacement and not a meal supplement, it's no wonder the only thing I got was slim results.

Personal Reflection & Group Discussion

Can you remember a time when you felt completely comfortable in your own skin?

Growing up, who or what shaped your definition of beauty?

2

WHATEVER IT TAKES

My freshman year of college, I gained about 10 pounds. Because I was still well within a normal and healthy weight range and having the time of my life, I wasn't all that concerned about it—that is, until one of my guy friends joked that I was "corn-fed" and "thick." I felt the heat rise to my cheeks as all the insecurities I ever had about my body and more flooded my mind. He must have read the emotion on my face because he quickly added that he meant it as a compliment… that I was athletic and strong. But those were not the words I wanted to be described as, and that was the moment I vowed I would lose weight… *whatever* it took.

I increased my daily workouts and decided to go on a high-protein diet. It wasn't very healthy because what I was eating was usually the cafeteria variety of chicken fried steak, hamburger patties, and hotdogs. But because I lost a few pounds, I was convinced I was on the right track to a slimmer and sexier me.

My sophomore year, I joined a sorority and moved into the house with 50 other young women. One evening as I was getting ready to go out, my lip gloss fell on the floor and rolled underneath my roommate's bed. As I felt around to retrieve it, my hand pressed down on a plastic bag with something warm and squishy in it. Curious, I opened the bag and nearly gagged at the sight and smell of her vomit. Disgusted, I quickly retied the bag and shoved it back under her bed.

I don't know what I expected a person battling an eating disorder to be like, but it wasn't like my roommate. That fact alone made me wonder how many other girls I knew were hiding the same secret. Not knowing what to do, I said nothing and simply observed her behavior. She went to the bathroom almost immediately after every meal, and it was always the single bathroom on the first floor… not the community one we all shared upstairs. She also ate the high-calorie foods I wouldn't allow myself to touch, went out drinking several nights a week, and never seemed to gain a pound. It seemed totally unfair, and what started as concern for her health began to turn to envy.

Determined to lose more weight, I decided to eliminate carbohydrates and do at least an hour of cardio each day. This would work for a few days, but then in a moment of weakness, I'd overindulge and eat a bunch of brownies or cookies. I'd feel terrible and recommit to my diet, but inevitably, the same thing would happen again a few days later.

It was after once such slip up when I was feeling particularly depressed that I remembered my roommate's secret. In just a few minutes, I could eliminate all the excess calories I had consumed and wouldn't have to worry about gaining an ounce. I sat on my bed contemplating what I was about to do. The thought of throwing up seemed awful, and I knew it was wrong, but I was desperate to lose weight. *It'll just be this one time,* I told myself. And with that rationale, I slipped down the stairs to the private bathroom and locked the door.

My heart began to beat faster as I knelt on the floor in front of the toilet. With fingers shaking, I opened my mouth and tried to stick them down my throat. The moment they grazed the back of it, I gagged and dry heaved. Nothing. I tried again with the same result and couldn't help but cough. I stopped and listened for the sound of any footsteps or voices outside as my heart pounded even harder in my chest. After I was sure nobody was nearby, I tried again and vomited up a little bit. My whole body shuddered in disgust.

My fingers were covered with spit and the remnants of my last meal, so I used the back of my arm to wipe the beads of sweat that were forming on my forehead. I looked into the toilet and realized what I had thrown up was probably the equivalent of only three bites of food. *You're going to have to do a lot better than that,* I told myself. So, I tried again and again, desperate to purge myself of the food I had eaten that I was convinced would make me fat and, therefore, unattractive.

When my eyes were so watery I couldn't see clearly and the back of my throat burned with the acid of my stomach, I gave up. I flushed the toilet, hoping that as the contents of my stomach disappeared so would my feelings of guilt. My hands were still shaking as I washed them, and though I tried to rinse my mouth out and gargle with water, I couldn't eliminate the putrid taste of vomit that lingered. When I finally looked up into the mirror, I did a double take. My skin was red and splotchy, my nose was running, and my eyes were bloodshot. As I tried to pull myself together so no one would know what I had just done, the gravity of my actions began to sink in. Now, I had a little secret, too.

Personal Reflection & Group Discussion

Have you or someone you know struggled with an eating disorder or a body-image issue?

What effects has that had in your life or the life of someone you know? (Consider self-confidence, physical health, relationships with others, etc.)

3

THE LIE

My decision to experiment with bulimia didn't happen overnight. It started years earlier when I chose to believe a lie. Of course, I didn't recognize this lie or realize how dangerous it was. But like a weed, it had grown to consume more and more of my thought life, and by the time I was sticking my fingers down my throat to throw up, this lie had all but strangled the truth in my mind.

This root lie, "I'm just not good enough," had spawned off into, "I'm not thin enough," "pretty enough," "tan enough," and so on. Without questioning where those thoughts had come from, I accepted them as the truth, but they were far from it. The truth was that my body was divinely made in the image of God, my self-worth was based on more than the numbers on the scale or the size of my jeans, and the color of my skin didn't determine my beauty.

The truth had the power to set me free, but I had been deceived by a lie that seemed to shout louder and louder in my head: *There's nothing wrong with doing whatever it takes to be beautiful. You'll look and feel amazing when you lose 10 pounds!* Because I genuinely believed that outer beauty mattered most, I justified my actions to attain it.

Despite the repulsiveness of throwing up, I tried it again a few weeks later after another slip up on my diet. Only this time, I didn't feel as bad about it. A week later, I did it again. By the fourth time, I started to think I had found the solution to my weight-loss struggle. I would still follow my regimented diet, but if I messed up or overindulged on occasion, I would have a backup plan. But what I thought was a solution was the slippery slope of a serious problem.

Because purging could rescue me from the effects of binging, I began to do so more frequently. I was getting better at eliminating the food, but I could never quite eliminate the guilt. Every time I finished, I'd feel ashamed and tell myself, *Ok, this is the last time. You're just going to have to eat perfectly from here on out.* But this self-induced pressure only made me more obsessed with food, and the more I tried to control my eating, the more it seemed to control me.

My whole life started revolving around what, when, and where I would eat. I would also analyze the habits of the women around me, and it wasn't long before I could easily spot those with eating disorders. Sometimes, it was what they ate or what they didn't eat. Mostly, I could tell by the way they looked at their food and everyone else's. I could see them comparing themselves, evaluating their options, and battling not only their own will power but also the lie that had them convinced that, to be beautiful, they had to be thin. I looked at food the same way, and I was losing that exact battle because I didn't know how to fight back. And without being armed for battle, I became more and more defeated and controlled by a lie that had grown into a viscous eating disorder.

One day, I walked into the community bathroom upstairs and heard an unmistakable sound coming from one of the stalls. It stopped immediately when the girl realized she was no longer alone. I quickly returned to my room to avoid the embarrassment of seeing her face to face. But I recognized her shoes and knew exactly who she was. I wasn't surprised. This girl was thin as a rail, ate like a horse, and was always disappearing to the bathroom after meals. On top of that, her skin was bad, and her hair was thin and dry… undoubtedly from lack of proper nutrition.

As I sat on my bed, it dawned on me that, if I continued down this course, I could easily end up like this girl. Throwing up a few times a week could quickly turn into throwing up a few times a day. And while tooth decay, bad breath, and poor skin and hair would certainly diminish my beauty and could lead to health problems down the road, that wasn't my biggest concern. The truth was that I felt like a prisoner held captive by my constant obsession with food, eating, and my body image. I was so consumed with my bulimia that I couldn't even enjoy food anymore. In fact, I hated it. I felt like I was spinning out of control on a not so merry-go-round that kept speeding up. And I was afraid that, if I didn't get off now, there would come a day when I would no longer be able to.

I felt completely incapable of stopping the binging and purging on my own. After all, I had wanted to do so many times before and hadn't been successful. I knew I needed God's help, but I was ashamed and didn't know what to say to Him. Cringing, I thought back to the times I had eaten so much food my stomach had ached, only to waste it all by throwing up. I didn't want to think about the fact that God knew and had seen the many times I had abused my body, the body He had given to me.

Not knowing where to start, I took a deep breath and said out loud the first thing that came to my mind. "God, I'm sorry..." I started to cry. "I know what I'm doing is wrong. And I don't want to do it anymore, but I need Your help."

When the tears finally dried up, I felt more hopeful than I had in months. Bringing God into the situation gave me the reassurance to believe I could live according to what the Bible said: "So whether you eat or drink, or whatever you do, do everything for the glory of God" (1 Cor. 10:31).

I resolved that I would not throw up, regardless of what I ate. As long as purging was an option, I knew the destructive cycle would never end. Thankfully, I was able to overcome bulimia before it overcame me. But my body-image struggle was far from over. It was like the lie, the nasty weed that had invaded my mind, knew I was trying to cut it out. In many ways, I had. I had cut out the obvious problem, the binging and purging. But I had failed to address the root issue which was that, at my core, I still believed I wasn't good enough. And because I didn't eradicate this lie from its root, it quickly grew back, convincing me that I needed to find some other way to attain the body I so desperately wanted.

Exercise was the next best way to alter my body. There was no shame or guilt in that, no little secret to hide. But what was a good thing in moderation quickly became an obsession in my life. Going to the gym was already a nonnegotiable daily requirement, so when I ate poorly, I would go twice. And on rare occasions, when I felt especially unattractive or that I might have gained a pound or two, I would go three times. Our sorority house was a 30-second walk to the campus recreation center, which only made my addiction that much easier to satisfy. And with no accountability or anyone to answer to about my schedule, no one had a clue about my *exercise bulimia*... not that I would have called it that at the time.

Throughout the course of college, my weight fluctuated by about 20 pounds. But even at my lightest, I still wasn't satisfied. It seemed that, no matter the number on the scale, I never felt good enough. And if it wasn't my size and weight, I was critical of my skin color, complexion, hair, or some other feature. When I looked in the mirror, all I could see were the things I didn't like and wanted to change.

On top of being my own worst critic, I only exacerbated the situation by constantly comparing myself to other girls. *Why couldn't I have her flawless skin? Her gorgeous hair? Her hour-glass figure?* I'd size her up and then see how well I measured up. It was a completely skewed evaluation. I would overlook her imperfections and dwell on her best features but then dwell on my own imperfections and completely overlook my best features. Now, there is a recipe for feeling perpetually inadequate and insecure!

I wasn't trying to be the best and healthiest version of myself. I was trying to be the picture-perfect version of somebody else.

And not just one woman. I would combine all the best features of several women together and dream up what the "ideal Rachel" should look like in my head. Then, it was up to me to try to modify myself to look like this mythical woman. Looking back now, I see exactly why I was so unhappy and discouraged with my appearance. I was trying to attain a goal that was not only unrealistic; it was impossible.

There is no way to tally the countless and frustrating hours I've spent trying to change what I look like. That's not mentioning the depressing ones I've spent comparing myself to others and wishing I had been given something different. Add on top of that all the insecurity and tears. And let's not forget the money I've spent on countless beauty products. Bottom line: It has turned out to be one poor investment after another, financially and emotionally.

Personal Reflection & Group Discussion

What lies have you believed about your outer beauty?

What has believing these lies cost you?

4

THE TRUTH

I know how easy it to believe the lie that you're just not good enough. After all, we can't watch TV, listen to the radio, read a magazine, or drive down the highway without being inundated with commercials, product endorsements, and advertisements convincing us we need this or that to be attractive, sexy, and happy. Marketers want us to believe we're just not good enough so we'll spend money on their products. But God's message is quite different. Not only did He create us, "God looked at everything he made and found it very good" (Gen. 1:31). He didn't say we're "not good enough," or even that we're just plain "good." He tells us that we are "very good." And if the God of the Universe says so, why don't we take Him at His word?

With that said, if you're like me, you probably still have things about your body or appearance you don't love or want to change. In the next chapter, we'll dive into what to do about those. But for now, it's time to ditch the myth that you're just not good enough, regardless of what you look like. And that's because, until you learn to love and appreciate the body God has given to you, you'll never feel good enough—even if you take drastic measures to change it. An outward change may make you feel better about yourself initially, but true and lasting confidence comes from the inside out—not the other way around.

I had the braces, the nose job, and the fake tan. And even when I was training for a marathon and was down to 8% body fat—which is very dangerous for a woman—I still wasn't comfortable in my own skin. In fact, I felt just as insecure and self-conscious as ever. I know I'm not the only one. There are plenty of other people—gorgeous people—who have spent countless hours, effort, and money on Botox, plastic surgery, diet pills, and cosmetic products yet still are not happy because they continue to believe the lie that they are just not good enough.

Choosing to love the body he has given to you by understanding God's truth is the most important step to combating this lie. It's also much easier to do when you let go of unrealistic expectations or societal standards. It finally dawned on me that, despite my valiant efforts, I would never be a flawless beauty or look like the airbrushed photos of models in magazines. Even if I tried to, what was the standard, and when would enough be enough? No matter how many hours I spent sweating at the gym, my body would never be perfect. Plus, I was still facing two undefeated opponents: gravity and time. I can fight them all I want, but their effects are inevitable, even with lots of money and effort.

I wish I could say I came to those realizations in a month or a year. In truth, it took me the better part of a decade to recognize that I had been deceived by a lie that was harming me physically and emotionally. Only when I refused to believe it, stood on the truth, and got realistic about my expectations was I able to work toward a healthy self-image and relationship with my body.

Personal Reflection & Group Discussion

What unhealthy expectations do you need to let go of regarding your physical appearance?

What would change if you really believed God's truth that you are His masterpiece and that you are "very good" just as you are?

5

SOME PRACTICAL STEPS

Stop the negative flow.

Several years ago, I noticed when I looked at the seemingly perfect women in magazines that I inevitably felt depressed about my physical appearance and convinced I needed to change it. I know now that—with all the makeup, photo editing, and perfect lighting—these images aren't even real to begin with, but at the time, I couldn't help but compare myself to them.

In a moment of clarity, I canceled my magazine subscriptions and started consciously eliminating anything that was damaging to my self-worth. I'd simply turn off the TV, change the radio station, or sign off Facebook. Setting boundaries and limiting these influences helped me to gain more self-confidence, happiness, and peace of mind—not to mention more free time.

In addition to the media, I've found that people sometimes can say things that negatively affect my self-image. While critical words can sting, I've learned to take comments like these and ask myself two questions: 1) *Is what they are saying true and/or based on a genuine desire to help me?* and 2) *Is what they are saying based on their own insecurities?* If the answer to either question is yes, this person probably has good intentions and/or a poor self-image. Either way, I filter it all before God and ask Him to convict me of any area I need to change and to show me how to move forward with that person.

Sometimes, this means doing nothing or simply praying for that individual. Other times, I'm prompted to have a conversation about how their comments have affected me. On a few occasions, God has led me to limit the time I spend with that person or to end the relationship all together. The idea isn't to label a person or write off anyone who has ever said something hurtful to you. It is about setting healthy boundaries, being aware of toxic people, and limiting the destructive influence they can have on your self-worth.

Finally, I would be remiss if I didn't address the biggest culprit when it comes to things that sabotage our self-confidence: *ourselves*! We tell ourselves things we would never think of telling another person... things like *You're so fat and ugly*, or *You'll never attract a man looking like that*. The scary thing is that, most of the time, we aren't even aware we are doing it.

It's time to stop being our own worst critic. While that won't happen instantly, become more conscious of your inner monologue. The next time it turns critical, do what I do and say, "Stop beating yourself up!" Then, stop! You may need to do this 10 times or more throughout the day, but even if you only do so twice, that's a step in the right direction. Over time, you'll get better and faster at stopping yourself when you are engaging in destructive self-talk.

Start the positive flow.

Once you limit the flow of negative influences, you must intentionally replace them with a steady stream of positive ones. When I need a self-esteem boost or a reminder of who I am, I turn to the source of all truth, the Bible. I read verses like...

> You formed my inmost being; you knit me in my mother's womb. I praise you, so wonderfully you made me; wonderful are your works! (Psa. 139:13-14)

Such verses remind me that I am wonderfully made. And the more time I spend reflecting on what God says, the easier it is to love and respect myself.

Another thing I've learned is that our words are incredibly powerful and we can use them to our advantage! A while back, I made a list of what I liked about myself and posted it on my bathroom mirror. Reading that list out loud each morning not only helped me to stop dwelling on the things I was self-conscious about, but it shifted my focus to appreciating my best features and qualities. This simple strategy transformed my self-image and was an awesome start to my day.

Of course, we all have things about ourselves that we are not necessarily thrilled about. When I find myself zeroing in on those areas or feeling bad about them, I ask myself, *Is this in my control, and is it reasonable to change?* If so, I consider healthy and realistic ways to do that. But if it's a God-given trait or condition and change would be detrimental or require extreme measures, I decide to let go and learn to live with it. When I work to improve upon what is appropriate and God-honoring to change, accept, and embrace the things that aren't, I am much happier and healthier.

Beyond myself, I also make a point to affirm others. I love watching someone light up and smile when I pay them a compliment. Besides brightening my day and hopefully theirs, doing so has other benefits: some of my closest friends today are women I met when I took the time to pay them a compliment.

And regarding friends, I make a point to surround myself with good ones! True friends love and accept me for who I am while also challenging me to grow and become the best and healthiest version of myself.

Implement tangible action steps to improve your health and beauty.

Taking the necessary steps to stop the negative flow and increase the positive flow of influences in your life is important, but we must also honor and care for the body God has given to us.

> Do you not know that your body is a temple of the Holy Spirit within you, whom you have from God, and that you are not your own? For you have been purchased at a price. Therefore, glorify God in your body. (1 Cor. 6:19)

Properly caring for our body not only glorifies God, but it's in our best interest. After all, our body is our vehicle through life, and it needs to last as long as we do!

It's taken years, but I finally have a healthy and balanced approach to my diet. No longer enslaved to calorie counting and obsessing about the number on the scale, I eat fresh, healthy food 80% of the time and allow myself liberty the rest of the time. Not only does this give my body the proper fuel to perform well now and for years to come, it allows me to enjoy a wide variety of foods without feeling like I need to deprive myself or overindulge. That makes eating so much more fun!

I continue to work out consistently, but I do so in moderation and with a different motivation. Rather than striving to have the thinnest or hottest body, I exercise to stay in shape, boost my energy, reduce stress, and sleep more peacefully.

Yes, life is busy, and it's easy to make excuses about our diet and exercise, but both are vitally important to you and those who love you! Obesity is an epidemic that is radically affecting not only the longevity of our lives but the quality as well. We are not meant to eat diets of highly processed, sugary foods in huge portions. Nor are we meant to be sedentary beings who sit behind a computer all day only to come home and sit in front of a television all night. We need fresh food, right-sized portions, and consistent physical activity so we can stay healthy, enjoy our lives, and be around for our children and grandchildren.

Beware of fad diets or "miracle" solutions. It takes both time and discipline to be healthy physically just as it does to be healthy emotionally. And it's important to note that the two are interconnected. You can look incredible on the outside, but if you still believe you aren't good enough, you'll continue to struggle with a poor self-image. On the other hand, speaking positively about your body image but neglecting your physical health doesn't honor you or God. Beliefs and actions must be congruent. And when they are, you'll not only be the best and healthiest version of yourself, but you'll feel amazing, too!

Personal Reflection & Group Discussion

*What one thing do you need to **stop** doing right now to improve your health and/or self-image?*

*What one thing do you need to **start** doing right now to improve your health and/or self-image?*

6

A CHANGED PERSPECTIVE

Once I began to see and honor my body in light of God's truth, my perspective on physical beauty changed. In the past, I thought that the thinner a woman was the more beautiful she was. It didn't matter that she looked like prepubescent teen; the smaller the number on the scale and size of clothing, the better. Far more attractive to me now is a woman who embraces her body, whatever the size, and treats it like the temple it is.

There was a time when I thought handsome men had to look like the models on the cover of *Men's Health*. While I can certainly appreciate nice physiques and rock-hard abs, they aren't nearly as impressive to me as before. Far more attractive than the guy who eats nothing but protein and spends all day in the gym is the one who is fit, self-confident, and knows his self-worth is based on more than how big his biceps are or how much weight he can push around.

I used to think that, the more polished and perfect a woman appeared to be, the more beautiful she was. Far more attractive than the woman who wears layers of makeup, self-tanner, fake eyelashes, and spends two hours getting ready every day is the one who isn't afraid to let her natural beauty shine. She may still enjoy getting made up, but she isn't afraid to let people see her when she's not.

Finally, I used to think beauty required eternal youthfulness and that, once you moved past your twenties and thirties, it was all downhill after that. While I'm not eagerly awaiting the effects of aging, I'm no longer dreading them. I want to cherish each day and live life without obsessing about what I'm going to look like in a few years or a few decades. Far more beautiful than the woman convinced she needs cosmetic surgeries, lifts, tucks, and pulls is the woman who loves herself—wrinkles and all—and sees them as the marks of wisdom and the blessings of a long life.

Does that mean that I ooze self-confidence 24/7 no matter what I look like or what others say? No. I'm still a human being with an innate desire to be attractive, and I live in a fallen world. But I'm a lot closer now than I've ever been, and if I can get to this place after battling all my insecurities, there is hope for you, too! You can have victory and freedom over things that used to enslave you and confidence in areas you were once insecure about. Life is so much more fun when you learn to love the body and skin you're living in!

Personal Reflection & Group Discussion

How can you broaden your definition of beauty beyond what society tells us is beautiful?

How would doing so affect your self-confidence?

7

UNFADING BEAUTY

While I hope and pray you learn to love and honor your body, that's not the whole picture when it comes to beauty. And that's because what truly makes us attractive as people goes way beyond external appearance. It's based on what's inside.

> Not as man sees does God see, because man sees the appearance, but the Lord looks into the heart.
> (1 Sam. 16:7)

I used to place so much value on the outward appearance that I was envious of beautiful people and naturally assumed they were somehow better than me. But when I began to see myself and others through God's eyes, I realized that He cares much more about our hearts than what we look like or the clothes we wear.

> Your adornment should not be an external one: braiding the hair, wearing gold jewelry, or dressing in fine clothes, but rather the hidden character of the heart, expressed in the imperishable beauty of a gentle and calm disposition, which is precious in the sight of God. (1 Pet. 3:3-4)

No matter what people look like on the outside, what is on the inside—their personality, character, and heart—will eventually shine through. That can either greatly magnify their beauty or dramatically diminish it. I know several people who wouldn't necessarily be described as exceptionally beautiful by society's standards, but their personality is so positive and magnetic and their heart so pure and loving that their internal beauty outshines their appearance, making them incredibly attractive.

One of my best friends fits this description perfectly. She is the kindest, most positive, and most generous person I know. In all the years I have known her, I've never heard a negative or condemning word come out of her mouth about anything or anyone. She is confident and has a laugh that is absolutely contagious. Because she loves God and others with all her heart, you can't help but want to be around her. There is no doubt she is the most beautiful person I have ever met.

I want to be this kind of person. Not only is she pleasing to God and attractive to other people, she has cultivated the kind of beauty that doesn't fade over time. It's the innate appeal of someone who is selfless, encouraging, and loving. It's the allure of someone who is authentic and is comfortable in his or her own skin. It's the unparalleled radiance of someone whose heart is full of hope, peace, and joy.

Isn't that wonderful news? I find great hope in knowing that the most important and endearing aspect of our attractiveness as human beings is not left up to chance or based on our family genetics. The true and eternal essence of feminine and masculine appeal begins and ends within. And unlike fleeting external beauty, internal beauty not only lasts forever but, when cultivated, makes us more and more attractive over the years… no matter our age, weight, or outward appearance. Now, that's the kind of beauty I can hope in!

Personal Reflection & Group Discussion

Who do you know whose internal beauty really shines?

In what ways can you cultivate your internal beauty?

8

TANGIBLE TAKEAWAYS

Let go...

Let go of negative self-talk.

Ask God to make you aware of any self-condemnation and to give you the strength to stop this bad habit. As often as necessary, say out loud or to yourself, *Stop beating yourself up!*

Let go of unrealistic expectations about your body.

Limit or cut out the negative influences affecting your self-image. Consider the input you've been receiving from social media, television, movies, magazines, and toxic relationships.

Let go of the lie that you're not good enough, thin enough, pretty enough, etc.

Write these lies out on a piece of paper, considering the pain and damage they have cost you. Refuse to believe them, and show your resolve by ripping up the list and throwing it away.

Be open to change...

Get a journal.

Journaling is one of the most powerful ways to express your emotions, dialogue with God, and grow. Not only will it help you process the past, embrace the present, and plan for the future, but when you look back, you'll be able to see all the progress you have made.

Do one thing every day to enhance your physical beauty.

Consider exercise, diet, grooming, etc. Journal about your commitment and results. What positive impact are these changes having in your life?

Do one thing every day to enhance your internal beauty.

Consider doing a random act of kindness or cultivating a virtue like patience, selflessness, or generosity. Journal about your commitment and results. What positive impact is this having in your life? How about in the lives of others?

Walk by faith…

Reflect on what God says about your identity and what is truly beautiful in His eyes.

> Charm is deceptive and beauty fleeting; the woman who fears the Lord is to be praised. (Prov. 31:30)

> Not as man sees does God see, because man sees the appearance, but the Lord looks into the heart. (1 Sam. 16:7)

> God looked at everything he had made, and he found it very good. (Gen. 1:31)

> You formed my inmost being; you knit me in my mother's womb. I praise you, so wonderfully you made me; wonderful are your works! (Psa. 139:13-14)

> Your adornment should not be an external one: braiding the hair, wearing gold jewelry, or dressing in fine clothes, but rather the hidden character of the heart, expressed in the imperishable beauty of a gentle and calm disposition, which is precious in the sight of God. (1 Pet. 3:3-4)

Write some or all of these verses above in your journal.

Which ones really speak to you? What do you think God is trying to tell you about your self-worth or external beauty? Journal your responses.

Write a personal prayer in your journal, committing to loving and honoring your body.

As an alternative to or in addition to writing your own personal prayer, you could also re-write the following:

> Heavenly Father, thank You for creating me in Your image. Help me to see myself through Your eyes and truly love myself. Please also help me to manage my time and make good decisions so I can care for my physical body and cultivate my internal beauty in a way that will honor and glorify You and make me the best and healthiest version of myself.

Forgive...

Forgive yourself for the times when you haven't honored or glorified God with your body or when you've engaged in negative self-talk.

Journal about your resolve to stop being your own worst critic and to stop any destructive behaviors that are affecting your physical or emotional health. Ask God for help, and if need be, reach out to a counselor or medical health professional for additional support.

Forgive yourself for the times you have judged or been critical of another person's external appearance.

If you have done or said anything that could be perceived as hurtful, offer an apology, and ask for forgiveness.

Forgive others who have criticized your body or appearance.

Write a note in your journal, asking God to help you let go of any bitterness toward them and to heal the pain in your heart.

Learn to love...

Learn to love yourself by making a list of at least 10 positive qualities about your physical appearance and internal beauty in your journal.

If you need help with this, ask a friend or a loved one what he or she most admires about you. Once you have compiled your list, make a copy, and post it in a place where you will see it every day (e.g. your bathroom mirror, the dashboard of your car, or on your refrigerator). Read this out loud every day to bolster your self-confidence.

Learn to love others by noticing and complimenting at least one person every day on either that person's external or internal beauty.

Record your results in your journal. How does this positively impact you? How does it impact the other person?

Learn to love yourself by celebrating the positive steps you are taking to enhance your internal and external beauty.

Consider buying a new outfit, hosting a get-together with friends, or just taking some quiet time to acknowledge your efforts. Life is too short not to celebrate, and you're worth it!

Part 2

HOPING IN SUCCESS

9

WHAT IS MY DREAM?

Countless times as a child, I was asked, "What do you want to be when you grow up?" My answer changed often. Back then, I wasn't worried about managing my reputation, maintaining job security, or planning for retirement. There was no fear of failure weighing in the back of my mind, and as far as I was concerned, anything was possible. Maybe that's why, over the course of my childhood, I wanted to be a fashion designer, artist, teacher, singer, aerobics instructor, and an actress. But while I might not have been able to nail down specifically what I was going to do, at 10 years old, I told God, "I want to do something *big* with my life." And I meant it.

As a typical middle child, I was always competing with my older sister and younger brother for my parents' attention as well as everybody else's. I loved to demonstrate my athletic prowess to anyone who would watch by showing off my running, gymnastic, bike-riding, and hula-hooping skills. Or, I would pretend I was on stage giving a stellar performance. If I knew the lyrics to a song, I would sing it. If there was a beat to be found—even if it was the rhythmic rumble of our old dryer in the laundry room—I would dance to it.

My dad lettered in four sports in high school and went on to major in physical education in college where he met and later married my mom, a piano major. I'd like to think I got the best of both of their talents, but while I played flute and basketball for several years, I wasn't great at either of them. It wasn't until I discovered musical theater my sophomore year of high school that I found my niche.

Because I could sing, dance, and act, I was cast as the Fairy Godmother in *Cinderella* and later as Lucy in *Charlie Brown*. It was my first time performing on a real stage, and I loved every minute of it. There was something magical about the bright lights, the costumes, the makeup, and the dusty, wooden smell of the old downtown theater we performed in. Right before the curtain would go up, I'd stand in the wings with my knees shaking and heart pounding like a hammer in my chest. The butterflies in my stomach would disappear after I recited my first few lines. Then, it was just pure bliss. I relished hearing the audience laugh, the sound of their applause, and watching hundreds of smiling people rise to their feet in a standing ovation at the end.

My voice wasn't strong enough for Broadway, but I could act. So, at 17, I decided to do something "big" with my life by moving to Los Angeles to become a famous actress. My plan was to break into the entertainment industry by doing soap operas and then cross over to do movies. Considering the number of hopeful stars who move to Hollywood and end up waiting tables, my parents were concerned. They encouraged me to apply for college but told me that, after graduation, I was free to do what I wanted.

We moved just north of Dallas, Texas for my last two years of high school, and I got involved with the drama department. Despite being a lead in two musicals in my previous arts magnet school, I couldn't seem to land a primary role in any of the productions at my new school. Disappointed but determined to find another way to make my dreams come true, I responded to a radio commercial for an acting and modeling agency in Dallas that was looking for new talent. I drove to the city for the initial consultation, which included reading a few lines and walking up and down a makeshift runway along with a dozen or so other hopeful stars. I did my best, prayed like crazy, and received a call back for a second interview. This time, my mom came with me.

I was asked to read through a short television commercial on video which I did with as much flare and gusto as possible. About 20 minutes later, the agency director invited me and my mom into her office. Sitting down behind her desk, she said nothing as she scanned over my resume and headshots, her face expressionless.

"I'm assuming this was your first time doing a camera read through?" she finally asked.

I nodded and swallowed the lump in my throat.

"You almost blew me away with the volume of your voice," she said. "This is television, not theater, so you don't need to project so much."

I nodded again, inwardly kicking myself.

"That said," she added, "you have a strong presence and a lot of potential. You need some work and polish, but I am willing to offer you a spot in this agency."

I felt like I'd just won the lottery. While my mom asked the practical questions about the time commitment, cost, and what sort of results I could expect, I envisioned myself in a gorgeous gown with flawless hair and makeup receiving my Emmy or Golden Globe. My thoughts wandered to the life of luxury I would lead, the handsome actors I would date, and the dreamy, steamy Hollywood heartthrob I would marry one day. We'd live in a beautiful mansion in Beverly Hills, be multi-millionaires...

"You said it cost $3,000?" my mom asked. I snapped back to reality and almost choked at the steep price. The woman nodded. I held my breath as I looked at my mom with pleading eyes. "We'll need to talk to your father about this," she said to both of us.

My mom told the owner we'd give her a decision by the end of the week, and we headed back home. Though she seemed fairly supportive, I knew the ultimate decision would be determined by my father. I spent the next few hours nervously pacing in my room as I waited for him to get home so I could present my case.

My dad thought I was joking when I first told him about the fee, but he listened sincerely and must have seen the passion in my eyes and heard it in my voice because he finally asked, "You really want to do this, don't you?"

"Yes!" I exclaimed.

He looked at me, nodded slowly, and said the word I had been dying to hear. "Okay."

I screeched with joy and hugged him, promising that when I was a rich and famous actress, I would repay him for this $3,000 investment with lots of interest. Despite their apprehensions about the entertainment industry, my parents were willing to sacrifice their hard-earned money and personal hopes and dreams for me so I could fully pursue my own. And that meant the world to me.

Over the next several months, I drove to Dallas each week to attend the acting and modeling classes that would help me become a star. But apart from modeling in a fashion show, the doors weren't opening. On top of that, my passion and excitement was starting to wane. I'm sure my lack of success had something to do with it, but when I thought of moving to L.A. to pursue acting and modeling fulltime, I felt uneasy and unsettled.

Because my parents had invested so much money for me to be part of this agency, I vowed to complete the entire program and give it my all. Each week, I prayed that if acting was God's plan for my life, He would either give me renewed passion and open a door of opportunity or at least confirm I was on the right path. Neither happened.

When the classes officially ended, I told my parents about my change of heart. They seemed relieved that a move to Hollywood was off the table and asked about my plans after high school. When I confessed that I wasn't sure, my dad spoke up. "Why don't you apply for an Air Force R.O.T.C. college scholarship and join the military?" he suggested.

I looked at him incredulously. "Uh, Dad… Can you imagine me in one of those uniforms?" I couldn't think of a worse fit for me than being in the Air Force or in any branch of service for that matter. I was someone who had always marched to the beat of my own drum… not to some military bugler. I liked being creative and standing out, not following rules and conforming. I valued freedom and doing things my own way. I didn't like anything or anyone that tried to control me or tell me what to do. Not to mention, I was confident I would look like an absolute dork in an R.O.T.C. uniform.

But because my dad had been so generous in supporting my acting dream, I decided to at least apply for the scholarship. I progressed through several rounds of qualifications, and a few weeks after a formal interview, I received a letter in the mail congratulating me on winning a four-year, complete Air Force R.O.T.C. scholarship to the school of my choice. While my parents were thrilled and I was honored to have won the scholarship, the thought of accepting it almost felt like a prison sentence. I was tempted to turn it down until I learned that I could get a free year of college with no financial or military service commitment if I quit the R.O.T.C. program after my freshman year. With that rationale, I decided to make my parents happy and accept the scholarship for one year only.

"Don't write off the program before you give it a try," my Dad said. "You might end up really liking it."

I shook my head. "Don't get your hopes up."

I accepted the scholarship and spent the next few months considering which college I wanted to attend. After touring some schools in Texas with my best friend, Emily, my parents took us down to Baton Rouge to visit my older sister, Sara, and look at Louisiana State University during homecoming weekend.

While the majestic oak-tree-lined streets and impressive buildings and architecture were beautiful, what really caught my attention were the boys and the football. I had never seen so many handsome Southern men. When we went to Tiger Stadium for the game that Saturday night, I felt an energy, passion, and school spirit unlike anything I had ever experienced.

At halftime, five convertibles drove onto the field with a guy and girl riding on the back. I watched in awe and with a little bit of envy as they announced the members of the homecoming court and then crowned the king and queen. I had always wanted to fit in and be the popular girl in school. Unfortunately, growing up in a military family, just when I stopped being the "new girl," it was time to move again. I tried to imagine what it would be like to be a member of the court down on the field, but considering that only 10 students were selected from a pool of 35,000, I knew it was a pipe dream.

After the game, Sara took me and Emily to a bar teeming with hundreds of LSU students. We spent the next few hours laughing, singing along to our favorite tunes, flirting with boys, and dancing so much that we sweated off all the makeup we had so carefully applied earlier. By the time we left at 2 a.m., it was official. Louisiana State University had just taken the number one spot on my college prospect list. And it stayed there.

Personal Reflection & Group Discussion

What did you dream about doing or being as a child?

Did you pursue that dream? If not, why not?

10

WHAT PATH DO I CHOOSE?

E mily and I both committed to going to LSU, and we moved into the dorms that fall. I decided to major in public relations because I was outgoing, liked people, and most importantly, the only math requirement was a three-hour basic algebra course.

I wasted no time enjoying the freedom of college life, and I loved everything about LSU—except R.O.T.C. Embarrassed by having to wear the uniform two days a week to my military classes, I purposely did not schedule any others on those days. I'd even carry my uniform across campus and change inside the R.O.T.C. building right before and after class so no one else would see me wearing it.

Freshman year flew by, and that summer, I had to make a decision about my scholarship. Despite my disdain of the program, the thought of taking out loans and working multiple jobs to make ends meet like my sister did sounded even worse than R.O.T.C. I went back and forth for weeks and finally decided that a free college education was too good to pass up. Plus, with a four-year military service commitment after graduation, I knew at least I'd leave college with a guaranteed job and great benefits.

Without a passion to pursue or a dream job to try to land after college, I began looking for other things to entertain myself and keep me busy. Joining a sorority seemed like the perfect solution, so I pledged to become a member of Delta Gamma Fraternity. In

a matter of weeks, my calendar was full of a wide array of philan-
thropic opportunities, activities around campus, and plenty of social events.

On the surface, everything was going great. But after several
months, I realized there was a growing emptiness inside that I
couldn't shake. One morning as I stared at my reflection in the
mirror, something deep inside of me asked, *Is this all there is?*
Taken aback, I immediately assessed my life. I was living in the
sorority house, making perfect grades, going on lots of dates, and
never lacking for something fun to do. Yet, in that instant, I knew
exactly what I had been missing: a sense of purpose. I had forgotten all about my dream of doing something big with my life. I was
just living for the moment with no personal goals for the future
and no plans to achieve them. Feeling lost and not knowing what
else to do, I pulled out my Bible and came across Ephesians 5:17-
19:

> Therefore do not continue in ignorance, but try to un-
> derstand what is the will of the Lord. And do not get
> drunk on wine, in which lies debauchery, but be filled
> with the Spirit.

I didn't have a clue what God's will was for my life specifically, but it was clear that getting drunk and partying was not part
of it. Convicted, I decided to refrain from drinking any more alcohol until I turned 21. Because most of my social activities revolved
around going to bars, I started looking for a new place to hang
out.

A few days later, I bumped into a friend on campus who invited me to an event at the Catholic Student Center that night.
Though it was a vastly different experience than I was used to, I
really enjoyed it. The people were genuine and welcoming, and
we had a deep and meaningful discussion about life and faith and
how that played out on a college campus.

I started going to more events, and as the time I spent at church increased, so did my desire to learn more about Jesus and why the people who claimed to know Him and follow His teachings seemed so happy. I started reading the Bible more frequently and found myself wandering across campus just to spend some time in the sanctuary. There was a stillness and quietness there I couldn't find anywhere else. And it was there that I understood what Jesus meant when He said, "Peace I leave with you; my peace I give to you. Not as the world gives do I give it to you" (John 14:27).

I loved gazing at the light coming through the stained-glassed windows and listening to the soothing sound of water trickling ever so softly in the baptismal font. It was a place where I could just talk to God about what was going on in my life, ask for advice, or pray for people I cared about. Even if I could only stay for a few minutes, I would always leave feeling lighter, happier, and somehow, fuller.

Because I was always going to Mass, didn't drink, and wouldn't do more than kiss guys, some of my sorority sisters jokingly called me "Sister Sherburne" and teased that I was going to end up in the convent. I always laughed, but I couldn't help but wonder if maybe they were on to something. My faith was deepening, and because I had several friends who were contemplating the religious life, the thought had crossed my mind. I knew nothing about being a nun other than what I'd seen in *The Sound of Music* and *Sister Act*, but when invited to a three-day silent retreat, I decided to attend.

As the weekend approached, I started to get apprehensive. What if God was really asking me to be a nun? It was certainly a far cry from a Hollywood actress or an Air Force officer, but it wasn't out of the realm of possibility. Besides, it did fit perfectly into my dream of doing something big with my life. Who knew? Maybe I'd be the next Mother Teresa.

The retreat afforded me time to quiet my mind and heart and really connect with God. His presence seemed to be everywhere, and during times of prayer, I asked Him to help me be open to a possible call to the religious life.

On the last day, I went outside to the rose garden and knelt down before a statue of the Blessed Virgin Mary holding Jesus. I gazed up at her face, transfixed by the tranquility and love it conveyed. I thought of the fear she must have felt as a young girl, being told by an angel that she would become pregnant with the Son of God. Despite how crazy that must have seemed, she trusted God, surrendered her own will, and gave birth to the Savior of the world... changing everything for all of eternity.

While I was confident my calling was much less significant than that, I too wanted the faith to say yes to God. I took a deep breath, closed my eyes, and mustered the courage to ask the question that had been weighing on my heart for weeks. "God, do you want me to become a nun?"

My heart pounded as I strained to listen. I wasn't sure what to expect. Would it be a booming voice from Heaven or a flash of lightning? I received neither. All I could hear was the sound of birds chirping in the distance. I remained kneeling for several more minutes, waiting to hear or feel anything, but I got nothing. No fear or excitement. No definitive answer.

On the drive home, a few of my friends shared that, over the weekend, God had confirmed their calling to join the convent or seminary. As I listened, I couldn't help but feel a tad slighted. I had asked God a direct question and hadn't heard anything. I knew there wasn't an overabundance of nuns in the world, and I couldn't help but wonder why God didn't seem to want me to be one. Was I not holy enough? Was it just not the right time? Determined not to miss my calling, I spent the next few months praying regularly for confirmation. But I never got any.

The Bible says, "Many are the plans in a man's heart, but it is the decision of the Lord that endures" (Prov. 19:21). That was clearly the case for me. Strike one was becoming an actress. Strike two was becoming a nun. The only thing that seemed to be working out effortlessly was my path to joining the military, which was almost laughable considering I had no desire to be on it.

Personal Reflection & Group Discussion

When facing a choice about which path to take in your life, who or what influences that decision?

Have you ever found yourself on a path you didn't want to be on? What did you do? How did you respond?

11

A MENTAL MAKEOVER

As an Air Force R.O.T.C. cadet, I was required to attend a 28-day field training after my sophomore year of college. Similar to boot camp, field training was intended to sharpen future officers and weed out those not capable of handing the physical and mental challenges of military leadership. Not only was graduating a requirement to be commissioned as an officer, I would be required to pay back my entire college scholarship if I didn't. This was cause for major concern. I had only put forth the minimum effort required to pass my R.O.T.C. classes, and with my lack of passion, knowledge, and leadership experience, field training was going to be especially brutal for me.

The day I had been dreading for two years finally arrived. I flew to San Antonio, Texas on an absolutely scorching day in June. From there, I boarded a bus to Lackland Air Force Base with cadets from around the country. I couldn't stop thinking about all the horror stories about field training I had heard from upper classmen. Given the anxious faces around me, I could only assume they had heard something similar.

By the time we arrived at our destination, I was a ball of nerves. The doors of the bus opened, and a short, stocky drill sergeant with a brimmed hat climbed on board, introduced himself. He explained that, when he said "move," we were to stand up, get our bags, quickly exit the bus, and line up along the sidewalk outside. I breathed a sigh of relief. I had been expecting yelling, fear, and intimidation tactics. This guy wasn't so bad.

He turned to the cadet sitting in the first row of the bus. "Is that a book bag you're wearing?" he asked.

"Yes, Sir," the cadet replied sharply.

The drill sergeant got inches from his face and roared, "Where do you think you're going?! Sesame Street?!"

Instantly, a wave of panic and dread washed over me. "Move!" he shouted. The bus became a flurry of activity as he continued to bark, "I said *move*! Faster! Faster! Faster!" With great haste, we grabbed our stuff and fled from the bus as the shouting reached decibels I didn't think were possible for a human voice. I had never met such a terrifying person... until I stepped outside and discovered six more drill sergeants who were equally as menacing.

That was just the first five minutes of field training, and things went downhill from there. By the third day, I was convinced I had discovered Hell. I couldn't sleep and was constantly hungry because I could never seem to eat enough food in the eight minutes we had allotted for each meal. Marching around in the Texas heat all day was exhausting and became excruciating when I developed huge blisters on my feet. On top of that was the insane amount of push-ups, sit-ups, and other exercises we did all throughout the day. But worst of all was the non-stop yelling and perpetual feeling of stress that I could not escape. I hated that more than anything.

By the end of the day, I wanted nothing more than to relax in a long, hot shower. But because we only had a few minutes to get cleaned up and I was sharing the same showerhead with several girls, I rarely got more than 30 seconds under a direct stream of water. Forget shaving. I was lucky to have time to brush my hair and apply deodorant.

Physically, my body was there. But mentally, I was checked out. Daydreaming was my only escape, so whenever possible, I'd imagine myself laying by the pool, or I'd make up a dance routine in my mind to my favorite pop song. When there was too much going on to do that, I'd simply calculate the minutes and hours till the next meal or bedtime or the number of days till graduation when the misery would end.

Despite my effort to fly under the radar and simply graduate, my flight commander noticed I was just going through the motions and called me out in front of all my peers. "Where is your head, Cadet Sherburne? It doesn't seem like you really want to be here. Do you want to be here?!" he asked.

"Yes, Sir!" I lied. I was sure that nobody in the history of time had ever wanted to be in such a dreadful place.

"Then, you'd better get your head in the game and start acting like it!" he thundered.

That night, as I laid on the top rack of my bunk bed, I reflected on his words. There was no question that I loathed everything about field training. But I also realized I had a choice. I could choose to be dejected and disgruntled and feel sorry for myself for the next 25 days, which wasn't going to make the time go by faster or make the experience any better. The other option was to change my attitude, get over myself, and make the most of what I could out of my situation despite how unpleasant it was. The latter sounded like a better option, so I started brainstorming ways I could do that.

What I lacked in military skills I made up for in the ability to encourage others. And with a journal full of inspirational quotes and Bible verses, I was well equipped to do so. No matter how I felt, I decided I was going to remain positive, hold nothing back, and give field training everything I had.

At the end of the first week, I had a one-on-one meeting with my flight commander to identify my personal goals. One was to get a perfect score on the physical fitness test, which consisted of sit-ups, push-ups, and a two-mile run. This was a stretch because

I had never been able to complete all the pushups or beat the required run time. But I trained hard, pushed myself, and my physical fitness test score steadily improved each week.

Despite the additional stress and responsibility, I also stepped up as a leader in my flight and found the experience to be exciting and rewarding. With my new attitude and goals, I rediscovered something I had been missing for a long time: a sense of purpose. And with that, I felt focused and energized, and field training became a whole new experience.

It wasn't long before we bonded as a flight. Whether it was the sleep deprivation or just the need to relieve some stress, there always seemed to be something to laugh about. And laughter truly was the best way to take the edge off. The days started passing more quickly, and before I knew it, it was the last week and time for the final physical fitness test.

"Cadet Sherburne, are you going to max this test?" my flight commander asked in front of my peers.

"Yes, Sir," I replied. This time, I wasn't lying. I had yet to get a perfect score, but it was now or never, and I had no intention of leaving field training without attaining my goal.

With that said, my stomach was upset, and I was beyond exhausted. As we marched to the outdoor track where the test would be held, I began to pray silently. *God, I know you probably have a lot more important things on your plate right now, but if you could, I'd really appreciate some extra strength and stamina this morning.* I wasn't sure if God heard or even answered requests like that, but I knew I had asked Him to do His part. And now, it was my responsibility to do mine.

The whistle blew to begin the first exercise, and I bolted into action. Sit-ups were not a problem, and I easily completed the required number well short of two minutes. Next were the pushups. My spotter placed her fist on the ground under me, and I got into position. At the sound of the whistle, I began cranking out pushups, touching my chest to her fist each time. In the past, I had always run out of time, or my arms had given out before the two minutes expired. This time, I was relentless, and I completed 45 push-ups in less than a minute. Knowing my prior ability, my spotter looked at me dumbfounded when I finished. "What did you eat for breakfast?" she asked in disbelief.

The last event was the two-mile run. I lined up on the starting line, and when the horn sounded, I took off. The first mile wasn't too bad, and adrenaline powered me through most of it. But by the second mile, my legs were starting to feel like lead weights, and I was developing a serious side cramp. My body was screaming for me to slow down, but I knew if I did, I wouldn't get the score I needed to max the test.

God, help me, I prayed. One of my favorite Bible verses came to mind. "I have the strength for everything through him who empowers me" (Phil. 4:13). Almost instantly, I felt my body relax. My stride evened out as I focused on pumping my arms and breathing. Everything but the white track lines seemed to disappear as I propelled myself forward with newfound strength and endurance. *For the glory of God. For the glory of God. For the glory of God,* I told myself.

When I completed the eighth lap and crossed the finish line, I wasn't even aware of my time until I heard my flight commander call out, "Cadet Sherburne... 13:52... way to go!" I collapsed on the grass and put my head to my knees. To everyone else, it appeared I was catching my breath. And I was. But I was also thanking God. After all, the only way I could have beaten my previous two-mile-run time by 57 seconds was with some help from above. Later, when my flight commander and peers asked me how I had done so well, I didn't hesitate. "I asked God to give me supernatural strength and stamina," I said. And I knew He had.

My four weeks at field training challenged me physically, mentally, and emotionally more than I ever imagined it would. But much to my surprise—and that of everyone who knew me— I actually enjoyed it. In addition to getting a perfect score on my physical fitness test, a few days later, I graduated from field training as a "Distinguished Graduate," an award given to the top one or two cadets in each flight. I felt a deep sense of pride and accomplishment. Maybe being in the military wasn't my dream job, but succeeding and winning awards was something I could definitely get used to.

Personal Reflection & Group Discussion

Think about a challenging or unpleasant situation you have faced. How did you get through it?

What did you learn from that experience, and how did it change you?

12

SUCCESS ADDICTION AND ITS COST

Back at LSU for my junior year, I took my passion for leadership and poured myself into R.O.T.C., student government, the Catholic Student Center, and several other organizations on campus. I was making tons of friends and building an impressive collegiate resume. But I was so busy and overcommitted that I rarely had time to see my closest friends.

My senior year, I was selected as the Air Force R.O.T.C. Wing Commander and was responsible for leading our detachment of 100 cadets. Several peers encouraged me to apply for the LSU Homecoming Court because leadership and campus involvement was a major component of the selection process. I was chosen as one of the top 30 applicants and had to prepare a two-minute speech and be interviewed by a panel of staff and alumni during "selection night." The competition was steep, and at the end of the evening, I was selected as one of the top five women on the homecoming court.

We were told that campaigning of any kind was prohibited and would result in disqualification. The Homecoming King and Queen would be elected by the student body with each student able to vote one time online. We needed to fill out a short bio and have our picture taken by the professional photographer for the website. For the pictures, everyone else was wearing a business suit, but because I didn't have one, I wore my military service dress instead. I didn't think anything of it until the photographer looked me over and frowned. "Do you have something else you can change into?" he asked. When I told him no and asked why, he replied, "I just don't know if the students at LSU are going to vote for a woman in uniform."

Shrugging my shoulders, I replied, "Well, this is who I am. And if people don't vote for me because I'm in R.O.T.C. and I wear a uniform, then I guess I'm not meant to be the LSU Homecoming Queen." With that, I sat down, smiled for the camera, and thought nothing more of it.

Homecoming Week was packed with social events, TV interviews, a pep rally, and a parade. My favorite part was when we, as members of the homecoming court, performed our choreographed dance routine to "It's Raining Men" in front of 1,200 students; we brought the house down. But the most meaningful part of that week was being stopped as I walked around campus and getting emails from students I had never met before. Many thanked me in advance for my service to our country. Some commented on my involvement in the Catholic Student Center. Others let me know they had voted for me and hoped I would win. Apparently, my biggest fear as a freshman had been unfounded. Not one person told me I was a dork for being in R.O.T.C., and boldly living out my Catholic faith didn't seem to offend anyone either.

Nevertheless, not being a Louisiana native, the typical Southern belle, or a sorority girl, I knew I didn't stand a chance of being crowned LSU's Homecoming Queen. When I found out that nearly my entire family was driving or flying in to be there for the game, I tried to convince them they didn't need to come. But they insisted, and with my sorority sisters, I had my own fan club holding signs and cheering me on as I rode past the Delta Gamma House during the Homecoming Day Parade.

My mom had convinced me to buy a business suit which I changed into before the football game that night. Sitting in a designated section with my fellow court members, we were escorted down to get situated on our convertibles right before halftime. As we drove onto the field, I was immediately overwhelmed by the sea of people around me—more than 92,000. I thought back to the homecoming game I had attended four years earlier when being part of the court seemed like an impossible dream. It still felt surreal, but I did my best to smile and wave to the crowd as I took it all in.

After we completed a lap, the guy I was paired up with took my arm, and we walked out onto the field. We stood as the announcer's voice boomed throughout the stadium, introducing each of us by name. There was a brief pause before it was time to reveal the winners. When the name of the Homecoming King was announced, the crowd cheered wildly.

After he was given a scepter and the noise died down, the announcer continued. "Your 2003 LSU Homecoming Queen is…" I prepared to applaud enthusiastically for the girl who would win. "Rachel Sherburne!" he bellowed.

I stood there in disbelief. It wasn't until my escort squeezed my arm and whispered in my ear, "That's *you!*", that I even moved. Shocked, I stepped forward as the former Homecoming Queen placed the crown on my head. I was handed a bouquet of roses, and a dozen photographers began snapping my picture.

The next several minutes were a blur, but I remember seeing my parents along the sideline. When I finally made it over to them, they had tears in their eyes. I had time to give them a quick hug and kiss before heading to the Chancellor's Suite with the Homecoming King for the second half of the game. When it was over, I met up with my entire family outside the stadium, taking photos with them, friends, and even complete strangers who wanted to meet, congratulate, and pose with the new LSU Homecoming Queen.

After all the flurry died down, we walked back to the sorority house where I said goodnight to my family. As I climbed the stairs to my room, I realized that, while I had lots of acquaintances and had won the majority of votes on a huge campus, I had all but neglected the relationships with my closest friends. A few of them had sent congratulatory text messages, but no one invited me to join them or offered to help me celebrate… not that I could blame them. I was the one who had pulled away from them, consumed with my desire to succeed and to make a name for myself around campus. And I had. I got exactly what I thought I wanted. But as I took off my crown and washed my face, I didn't feel all that special or like royalty. I just felt lonely.

In addition to being the Air Force R.O.T.C. Wing Commander and Homecoming Queen, I was also named LSU's Most Outstanding Senior and the recipient of several other leadership, academic, and service awards and honors. My college career culminated with a commission as an Air Force officer. The following day, I got to meet and shake hands with President George W. Bush before he spoke at our graduation.

Though I had achieved the pinnacle of collegiate success, I couldn't help but feel something was missing. But rather than exploring and questioning that feeling, I stayed busy and prepared to move to Virginia to start my career as a public affairs officer.

***

My first assignment at Langley Air Force Base was to lead a small team and produce our 24-page weekly base newspaper. While not the greatest editor, I enjoyed meeting people from all over the base as I interviewed them and wrote articles. It was through one such connection that I learned about a unique opportunity: being a narrator for the United States Air Force F-15 East Coast Demonstration Team.

I didn't have any experience speaking at airshows, and I knew very little about fighter jets. But with my acting experience, I had no problem reading a script with lots of energy and enthusiasm. I auditioned and was selected to be part of the team. I began traveling to airshows around the world about two weekends a month from March to October. When the pilot was demonstrating the capability of the aircraft, I was the voice on the loud-speaker announcing his maneuvers and trying to drum up the crowd. "Ladies and Gentlemen, from your left, your United States Air Force F-15 Eagle!" I would shout into the microphone right before the jet whizzed by and drowned me out.

Being in the spotlight, speaking before millions, and traveling the globe with a precision fighter jet demonstration team would satisfy most people's egos, but when I wasn't holding the microphone at airshows, I was looking for other ways to prove my abilities.

Though I had never run more than five miles at once, I decided to sign up for the Air Force Marathon. I followed the rigorous training plan and completed 26.2 miles in 3 hours and 46 minutes, winning second place in my age category. For a few weeks, I enjoyed the sense of accomplishment, but it didn't last long, and I soon was looking for that next thing to dive into and dominate.

I enrolled in a master's program and started taking online classes while volunteering at the base chapel to lead a new young adult program through the military called "Catholics Seeking Christ." On paper, I was the epitome of the ideal Air Force officer, but my relentless drive for success was taking its toll. Fatigued, 20 pounds lighter, and disconnected from my close friends and family members, I had aged 10 years in the last two. My family voiced their concerns. They were worried about me and rightly so. But I was too stubborn to listen. I convinced myself that I would be happy when I won that next award or reached a new milestone. Over the next several months, the accolades continued to come, but happiness never did. And that's when I hit a low point.

Feeling particularly overwhelmed and lost, I called Sarah, a fellow public affairs officer who had taken me under her wing when I first arrived at Langley. Besides being an exceptional officer and mentor, she was a great friend and sounding board. Even though I hadn't seen Sarah in weeks and she was busy packing for a month-long trip to Egypt, she still spent an hour on the phone to listen to me and cheer me up. She always knew what to say, and by the time we hung up, I already felt better. I silently thanked God for Sarah's friendship and promised that, when she got back, I would be better about staying in touch and making time to be there for her as well. Unfortunately, I never had a chance to keep that promise. Two weeks later, while still in Egypt, Sarah was killed in a tragic car accident.

I was at work when I heard the news. It took several seconds for it to register. When it did, I felt sick to my stomach. I ran down the hall to the bathroom, trying to hold back the tears and vomit I felt rising in the back of my throat. *This couldn't have happened*, I thought, sobbing. *People aren't supposed to die this young and certainly not people like Sarah.*

For the next several months, I grieved for Sarah, her family, and myself. She was one of my closest friends at that time, yet I knew deep down that the relationship had been largely one-sided. I reached out to Sarah when I needed her. She met very specific needs in my life, but had I met any in hers? At night, the regret gnawed at me. I had prioritized my success over relationships, thinking that, when life slowed down one day, I would make those a priority. But now, I knew differently. Life wasn't slowing down, and I wasn't guaranteed tomorrow.

> You have no idea what your life will be like tomorrow. You are a puff of smoke that appears briefly and then disappears. (Jas. 4:14)

I found out later that, right before she left for her trip, Sarah had written letters to each person in her family, telling them how much she loved them. I wonder if she subconsciously knew that would be the last communication she would ever have with her family... her last opportunity to tell them how much they meant to her. Or maybe, God had prompted her to write them because He knew they would need those letters to cope with her death in the months and years to come.

Sarah's death forced me to consider how I was living my life. When I found out I would be deploying to Iraq a few months later, I found myself pondering some tough questions. *What if I don't make it home? Have I lived my life to the fullest and done what God asked me to do?*

> You shall love the Lord your God with all of your heart, with all your being, with all your strength, and with all your mind, and your neighbor as yourself. (Luke 10:27)

I loved God to some extent but knew my other relationships needed a lot of work. Determined to take a step in the right direction, I sat down at my computer and typed out a long letter to my parents. My eyes filled with tears as I remembered all their sacrifices and the countless ways they had supported me. They loved me more than I ever deserved, and while I was successful at many things in my life, I was failing not just as a daughter but also as a sister and a friend. I prayed for God to help me really learn how to love others and vowed that, from that point on, things would be different. I would be different.

Personal Reflection & Group Discussion

How has the desire for worldly success affected your life?

Have you ever gotten exactly what you thought you wanted, only to realize it didn't make you happy?

13

A NEW DREAM

arrived in Baghdad a few weeks after Saddam Hussein was executed and right as the troop surge in Iraq began in early 2007. It took some time to adjust to the 12-14-hour nightshifts but more so to deal with the sobering realities of war. I worked in the Joint Operations Center, which was the information hub of everything going on in Iraq. My job was to help send out press releases and answer questions from the media about IED attacks, deaths, and helicopter crashes—all of which were steadily increasing. I was also responsible for researching how the media worldwide was reporting on the U.S. and our operations. Three days a week, I briefed the three-star general and other senior leaders during our battle update assessment meetings.

I felt fortunate to be working in one of Saddam's former palaces on a relatively safe and secure military base, but other troops were patrolling streets and dodging bullets and IEDs in one of the most hostile and dangerous cities in the world at that time. Many were also on their second or third 12-15-month deployment. Even still, a single four-month deployment to Baghdad turned out to be a life-changing experience for me.

I walked into the base chapel that first Sunday, jetlagged and exhausted after being up all night working. Instead of my Sunday best, I was wearing my uniform, combat boots, and a 9-millimeter pistol on my hip. Sitting down, I glanced at the strangers around me and wondered how long they had been deployed. *Do they have spouses or children back home? Have they lost loved ones in this war? Would any of them be killed in the line of duty?* It occurred to me that I was sitting among the bravest and most selfless men and women in our country. Bowing my head, I silently prayed God would protect and bring us all home safely.

There was no choir, but after communion, the chaplain played a song on the portable CD player called "We Are One Body." I vaguely remembered hearing the song before, but the words had new meaning: "We are one body, one body in Christ, and we do not stand alone." An unexpected lump formed in my throat, and before I knew it, tears began to stream down my face. I realized that the people sitting around me were not strangers. They were my brothers and sisters in Christ, and to get through this deployment, we would need to support each other.

Sensing God's call to do something tangible, I prayed over the next week and felt led to do two things: 1) help start a church choir and 2) lead a Bible study. When I talked to the chaplain, he was overjoyed at my willingness to step up as a leader. He made an announcement the following Sunday and told interested people to talk to me after Mass. Several people volunteered to join the choir, and though I had no experience leading a musical group, I did my best.

Despite a few practices, our first performance the next weekend was pretty rough. After Mass, a two-star Air Force general pulled me aside and asked if he could join the choir and play his guitar. Regardless of whether he was offering to join our ranks out of a genuine desire to contribute or because we were so terrible, we were relieved to have him. And with his guitar skills and strong voice, we started sounding a lot better.

With the choir in place, I started facilitating the "Catholics Seeking Christ" program I had been trained to lead back in Virginia. Over the next six weeks, we had a diverse group of men and women of all ranks, ages, and branches of services who attended. Because each session was built around a video, I didn't have to do much, but I enjoyed asking questions, leading times of prayer, sharing my faith, and making new friends.

At the end of the six weeks, I received an email from a Marine lieutenant colonel who had participated in the group. He thanked me for leading the program and went on to say how much he had gained from the experience. *You helped facilitate a relationship with me and the "Big Guy," and it changed my life,* he wrote. I knew it was simply God working through me that had transformed this man's life. Even still, I felt something burning inside. It was an emotion I hadn't felt in a long time, something I had been missing for most of my adult life: passion.

Almost overnight, my life-long dream changed from me wanting to do something big with my life to inviting God to do something big *through* me. I started looking for ways I could be His hands and feet and to share the light of Christ with others. Sometimes, it was simply smiling and saying hello to the people I passed to and from work. Other times, it was chatting with the gate guards or people in line at the dining facility. I soon learned that asking "How are you doing today?" and waiting for the answer could lead to some great conversations, opportunities for prayer, or just a chance for people to feel valued and heard. It also energized me and lifted my spirits as well.

In four short months, I made stronger friendships in Baghdad than I had in four years of college. My new friends threw me a "Rachelpalooza" farewell party, and though I was sad to leave, I was returning home as a different person... a better person. My focus had shifted from striving for ways to succeed to searching for ways to serve, and I was eager to lead my team.

Mentoring my 10 Airmen truly brought me great joy, and I was disappointed a few months later when I got a new assignment. Professionally, it was a great opportunity, but as the youngest ranking officer in a joint service command, I knew my days of leading others were over... at least, for the time being.

As I cleaned out my office, I couldn't help but reflect on my three and a half years at Langley Air Force Base. The awards and medals I had worked so hard to win didn't seem nearly as valuable as I once believed them to be. While the job I had done was important, I realized that it wasn't the Air Force mission I was passionate about; it was the people. As I said my goodbyes to those I had worked with, I hoped that their lives were somehow richer because I had been a small part of them.

With my car packed, I headed straight to a weekend retreat hosted by my church. It just so happened to fall on the weekend I was transitioning between jobs and was a much-needed respite to pray and reflect. Though I was heading toward a promising military career, deep down, I couldn't help but wonder if perhaps God was calling me to something different.

The weekend further awakened my desire and passion for evangelism. Something came alive inside of me when I talked about God, shared stories of how He had been working in my life, and prayed with and for others. With all the religious sensitivities, boldly sharing my faith was not something I could do in uniform—at least, not openly.

On the last night of the weekend, we were asked to identify anything standing in the way of our relationship with God and where He was calling us to go. Once we had clarity about what we needed to surrender, we were told to write it down or find a tangible representation to offer to God by physically placing it in a box on the altar. After praying, I got what I needed from inside my car and knelt before the altar. I was fairly confident that I could continue on in the Air Force, retire, and have financial security for the rest of my life. But I knew that, in doing so, I'd be settling. I wasn't sure how to live out my dream of sharing the light of Christ with others and earn an income, yet I couldn't shake the feeling that God was asking me to let go and be open to something new.

My heart was pounding, but at the same time, I felt a deep sense of interior peace. What I held in my hand represented my financial security, everything I had worked so hard to earn and the only job I knew. I took a deep breath. "Alright, God…" I whispered, dropping my military dog tags into the offering box. "I'm yours."

Personal Reflection & Group Discussion

What are you passionate about?

Have you taken steps to pursue that passion? If not, why not?

14

TRAPS THAT KEEP US FROM PURSUING OUR DREAMS

My journey of chasing my dreams, seeking success, and uncovering my passion and purpose has had many unexpected plot twists. Looking back, I see several factors that have greatly affected it and could have derailed it. This is not to say that wanting a reliable job, working hard, attaining a respectable title, trying to minimize fears and failures, and desiring a nice paycheck are bad. They are not. But if left unchecked, those can become roadblocks or even traps that keep us from pursuing our God-given dreams.

The Comfort-and-Security Trap

We all have what I call a "comfort instinct." Without trying, our brains naturally direct us to avoid pain and maximize pleasure. The need for comfort goes right along with our need for security. After all, part of being comfortable is knowing we have a roof over our heads, food on the table, and protection from danger. Sometimes, this innate longing protects us from harm and unnecessary discomfort. Other times, it holds us back from taking the necessary risks to pursue our dreams.

If you've settled for a job that you aren't passionate about but you think, *I'd be crazy to give up this comfort and security to pursue my dreams*, I challenge you to reconsider. To me, it's crazy to settle for mediocrity when there is endless opportunity and potential for greatness, to have a burning passion but never do anything with it, and to spend hours each week watching celebrities act out scripted adventures on television and in movies but never get off the couch to pursue your own.

If you've fallen into the trap of comfort and security, I get it, and I've been there. But it doesn't mean things have to stay the same. Falling into this trap certainly won't kill you, but there's a good chance it will kill the dream inside of you, so I hope you avoid it.

The Workaholic Trap

We live in a society that often celebrates those who work the longest hours, even if it means working 60-80 hours a week at the cost of one's relationships, physical health, and emotional well-being.

Of course, there are times when extra effort at work is required. Maybe a project deadline is looming, you must fill in for a sick coworker, or it's just a busy stretch for the company. Those things happen and are normal in moderation. But if you regularly bring work home, struggle to unplug and relax outside of the office, or your job often takes priority over your family and health, I hope you will take some time to step back and rethink your priorities. Consider what all of this is costing you physically, emotionally, spiritually, and relationally. Then, ask yourself two questions: 1) *Is all my hard work helping me to achieve my dreams and live the kind of life I really want to live?*, and 2) *In 10, 20, or 30 years, will the benefits of all my efforts outweigh the cost?* If the answer to either or both questions is no, it's time to make a change.

The Title Trap

Having a title like *doctor, judge, general,* or *president* demonstrates competence and commands respect in the eyes of others. But if the title is all you're after, beware. I had many impressive titles throughout college and in the military, but none of them corresponded to my true passion and thus weren't truly fulfilling in the end. In some cases, they only further distracted me from my true calling because they came with increasing responsibility, time commitment, and stress.

Before you work toward any title, consider how well you are embodying the ones that truly matter, titles like *mother, father, sister, brother, wife, husband,* and *friend.* And if your dream is to hold some other impressive title one day, set the bar high and give it your all! We need great leaders and role models in every area of society. Just remember that success is not determined by a title. I have met some amazing people called *mom, janitor,* and *volunteer* who I respect and admire much more than some called *CEO, president,* or *commander.* After all, a title doesn't define you. You define your title, whatever that may be.

The Fear-of-Failure Trap

While nobody likes to fail and most of us try to avoid fear, there are actually benefits of both! When we are afraid, it's usually because we are doing something that is difficult or outside of our comfort zone. I was terrified to go to field training, but it sharpened my skills, pushed me past what I thought I was capable of, and uncovered a hidden passion that I didn't even know I had. Fear can be a sign that we're doing something good.

Every failure has the potential to bring you one step closer to success. You know who fails more than anybody else in life? Successful people! They weren't born into success. They failed their way there. And you can, too, if you have the right approach. Instead of beating yourself up, blaming others, or getting discouraged when you fail, accept personal responsibility, learn from your mistakes, apply what you've learned, and try again. Fail forward. If you will do this every time you fail, you'll keep making progress toward your goal.

Working through fear and failure will help to keep you humble, force you to learn new skills, and give you an opportunity to master your psychology. So, don't be afraid to fail forward. It'll make you a better and stronger person, and you'll never have to live with regret or wonder what could have been. You can be proud, knowing you gave your all to your dream. And you can't put a price tag on that.

The Money Trap

The final trap that keeps many people from pursuing their dreams in life is the quest for money or thinking they don't have enough. For a season, you might have to work a job you don't love to make ends meet. Just be careful that you don't lose sight of your dreams or wrongly assume that you can only pursue them if you have plenty of savings or a steady stream of income.

With that said, I'm not advocating quitting your job to start a business if you have no revenue or money in the bank—unless that's what God is calling you to do. In that case, listen to Him! But you can make progress toward your goals regardless of your financial situation. Reading books from a library is free, as is researching, brainstorming, talking to people, volunteering, and sometimes even getting hands-on experience. Do what you can to upgrade your skills, and refuse to compare yourself to anyone else. Some of the most successful people in the world started with nothing more than a dream and a burning desire to achieve it. Think outside the box, believe in yourself, and don't give up!

While a lack of money can certainly keep you from pursuing your dreams, so can having an overabundance of it. There are plenty of people working high-paying jobs and making tons of money while hating every minute of it. They often try to distract themselves with a new sports car, home upgrade, or the newest tech gadget that just came out. Unfortunately, money can't buy happiness. In fact, studies have proven that lottery winners and millionaires aren't any better off than the rest of us when it comes to fulfillment. Some of the most miserable people I know have millions while some of the most joyful are barely making ends meet.

The bottom line about the money trap is not that money is good or bad. It's that money should be the natural result of following your dreams and passions, not the reason why you never pursue them or why you settle for a job you despise just to make more of it. If you want to be a millionaire doing the thing you love, I hope you make more money than you have ever dreamed of and that you discover more passion and fulfillment, too! And if doing the thing you love means you'll never be well off financially, I would encourage you to do that as well! You'll be richer in other ways. I am convinced that we reap supernatural blessings in this life and the next when we follow our dreams and do what God has created us to do.

Personal Reflection & Group Discussion

What trap or "traps" have you fallen into as you seek success?

How have those "traps" been affecting your health, relationships, and willingness to live out your passions?

15

TRUE SUCCESS

I know now that success is much more than a fancy job, impressive title, or a big paycheck. It's about uncovering your passions and pursuing the dreams God has given to you. The Bible says, "For God is the one who, for his good purpose, works in you both to desire and to work" (Phil. 2:13). He gave your dreams and passions to you for a reason, and He wants you to pursue them!

With that said, if you're not totally clear about what your dreams and passions are, you're not alone. At a seminar I recently hosted, more than 75 percent of the attendees could not clearly identify their dreams. Some had been discouraged from pursuing them, given up on them, traded them in for comfort and security, or forgotten about them entirely. Over the next several hours, I led participants through a series of exercises in which they could pray, reflect, and get clarity about their passions and what God wanted them to do with them. At the end of the day, dozens of people approached me with bright eyes, excitedly telling me about their dreams and what steps they were going to take to pursue them. Their enthusiasm and joy were palpable.

I challenge and invite you to set aside some time to journal, reflect, brainstorm, and get clarity about your dreams. Once you have done that, take some practical steps toward making those dreams a reality. Maybe you need to buy a book, sign up for a class, plan a trip somewhere, or hire a coach. But do something, and keep an open mind. One of the biggest challenges many of my coaching clients face is that they don't dream big enough. They underestimate their abilities and what is possible while overestimating how difficult achieving their goals will be. Refuse to put limits on yourself, God, or what you think is possible.

This doesn't mean we will all accomplish our dreams in life. But I've come to believe that what's more important is actually pursuing them. It's in chasing our dreams that we learn invaluable life lessons, grow, and change in unbelievable ways. And it makes for some amazing stories. Just think about how many movies recount the tale of someone who persisted despite facing challenging obstacles... someone who wasn't afraid to follow his heart even if it led to unexplored territory... someone who boldly blazed a trail toward her dreams, no matter how impossible it seemed. We love to hear stories of those who sought hard after their God-given passions. Why? Because at the core of who we are, there is a burning desire to chase after our own dreams... no matter how dim that flame has grown over the years.

No matter your age or life experience, it's never too late to rediscover your passions, cultivate your talents, and do the thing that you love. Just remember that you can't buy your dreams, wish them away, or pretend they don't exist. You can only pursue them. And I hope you will.

Personal Reflection & Group Discussion

If money was not an issue and you knew you couldn't fail, what is the one thing you would be excited to get out of bed and do every day for the rest of your life?

If you found a way to pursue your passions, how would that change your life?

16

TANGIBLE TAKEAWAYS

Let go...

Let go of assuming you're too old to dream.

Take some time to journal and ask God to give you clarity about the passions and dreams He has deposited within you.

Let go of unnecessary distractions or habits that are keeping you from pursuing your dreams and passions.

It could be wasting time online, watching TV, or just making excuses. Write these in your journal, and decide which ones you need to limit and/or cut out completely.

Let go of negative self-talk about yourself or your dream.

Margaret Thatcher once said,

> Watch your thoughts for they become words. Watch your words for they become actions. Watch your actions for they become habits. Watch your habits for they become your character. And watch your character for it becomes your destiny. What we think, we become.

Be open to change…

Brainstorm creative ways to pursue your passions.

These opportunities could help you to start pursuing your passions part-time or as a hobby. Think outside the box and journal your ideas and strategies.

Read a book about your dreams and how to pursue them.

Put Your Dream to the Test by John Maxwell is a great place to start.

Seek mentorship or hire a coach.

A mentor or coach can help you to avoid costly mistakes, keep you focused, and help you achieve your goals and dreams more quickly and efficiently than you could on your own.

Walk by faith…

Spend some time reflecting on what the Bible says about pursuing your God-given dreams.

> Many are the plans in a man's heart, but it is the decision of the Lord that endures. (Prov. 19:21)

> For God is the one who, for his good purpose, works in you both to desire and to work. (Phil. 2:13)

> Those whose steps are guided by the Lord, whose way God approves, may stumble, but they will never fall for the Lord holds their hand. (Psa. 37:23-24)

Trust in the Lord with all your heart, on your own intelligence rely not; in all of your ways be mindful of him, and he will make straight your paths.
(Prov. 3:5-6)

For the Lord gives wisdom, from his mouth come knowledge and understanding; He has counsel in store for the upright, he is the shield of those who walk honestly, guarding the paths of justice, protecting the way of his pious ones. Then you will understand rectitude and justice, honesty, every good path.
(Prov. 2:6-9)

Thus says the LORD, your Redeemer, the Holy One of Israel; I the LORD, your God, teach you what is for your good, and lead you on the way you should go.
(Isa. 48:17)

Write a prayer in your journal asking God to confirm the dream or passion you should pursue.

You could also rewrite the following prayer:

Lord, please increase my desire to do that which You created me to do, and decrease my desire for anything that may distract me from that. Open doors of opportunity and guide me as I follow after the dream You have given me in a way that honors You.

Write in your journal as if you are talking directly to God. Be bold, and don't hold back from asking Him questions about your dreams, telling Him your deepest desires, and being honest about your fears and frustrations. As you reflect and listen, write down any thoughts, feelings, or visions you may have.

Forgive...

Forgive yourself for your past mistakes or decisions that have kept you from pursuing your dream.

Let go of past regrets, and refocus on moving forward.

Forgive others who have discouraged you from pursuing your dream or made you believe you couldn't succeed in life.

Write a note to God forgiving those people for their words and actions.

Forgive yourself for the times you have crushed someone else's dream or discouraged them from pursuing it.

If appropriate, ask for forgiveness or write a note of apology to this person and try to become a source of encouragement for them in the future.

Learn to love...

Learn to love yourself by setting goals and taking small, consistent steps toward pursuing your passions.

Every time you take a step forward, record your progress in your journal and celebrate your success.

Learn to love others by offering to help them pursue their dreams.

Consider writing a letter of recommendation for someone and/or volunteering your time to mentor someone who needs your expertise. You will reap what you sow, so give selflessly to help others, and trust that God will bless your efforts as well.

Learn to love yourself by making a list of all your unique talents and skills in your journal.

Think about your personality, education, communication ability, relational ability, technical skills, and/or athletic skills. Read over this list regularly to remind yourself you have something valuable to offer—especially at times when you're facing fear and self-doubt.

Part 3

HOPING IN SIGNIFICANCE

17

THE CALL

The Monday following the retreat, I reported to my new job. Whether it was being in a new office or simply having more clarity that my passion was changing, I got the distinct feeling that my days in the Air Force were numbered. The pace of the job was much less intense, so I doubled up on my course load and focused on completing my master's degree in Global Leadership and Entrepreneurship from Regent University.

For my final project in the master's program, a friend helped me to create a nine-minute video using some of the footage I had recorded during my deployment to Iraq. I called it "Light of the World" because it encapsulated what I had learned about servant leadership and my passion for sharing the light of Christ with others. The video won "Project of the Year," and I was invited to do a live television interview on the Christian Broadcasting Network. Shortly after the segment aired, I started receiving emails from people all over the world with a connection to the military or who were simply inspired by my video. As I read their messages, I couldn't help but feel God was preparing me for something different and amazing.

> For I know well the plans I have in mind for you, says the Lord, plans for your welfare, not for woe! Plans to give you a future full of hope. (Jer. 29:11)

A few weeks later, I received an email from a woman who had seen my video and had a similar passion. She worked for an international organization called Military Ministry whose mission was to support the spiritual needs of troops and families. She invited me to visit their headquarters. Given my passion for God and the military and that their office was less than three miles from my house, I eagerly accepted her invitation.

When I walked into the Military Ministry building, the first thing I noticed was the atmosphere. Peace seemed to permeate the entire space, and everyone I met exuded joy and seemed genuinely happy. They greeted me with warm smiles, bright eyes, and even some hugs before we assembled in their meeting room for daily devotionals and a time of prayer.

Someone read a short passage from the Bible, and afterward, the staff members discussed its application to their lives. Their genuine desire to understand and follow Christ's teaching amazed me. I yearned to work in a place where I could openly discuss my faith and be challenged and inspired to grow spiritually.

Next, the staff prayed fervently for the families of the three military chaplains who had committed suicide during the previous 18 months, for the many military couples on the brink of divorce, and for those struggling with post-traumatic stress disorder (PTSD), a growing epidemic plaguing the military. I knew many troops and families were struggling, but even I didn't realize to what extent. *What is being done to help them,* I wondered.

I was then given a tour and a brief overview of Military Ministry's strategic vision, resources, programs, and how they integrated faith into the healing process—something I knew firsthand that troops and families needed. When I asked how this 45-year-old ministry was practically in my backyard and I had never heard of it, the executive director looked at me and smiled, "Well, that's because we don't have someone with your public affairs skills helping us to get the word out." I knew my visit wasn't a random coincidence, and with my interest piqued, I accepted their invitation to return a few weeks later for a full-day preview of the ministry.

When I returned, I learned that not only was Military Ministry supporting U.S. troops and families in need, but they were also spreading the gospel to indigenous military leaders in 26 countries internationally. As I spent time with each member of the leadership team to understand the full breadth and scope of the ministry, the excitement was building inside me. By the end of the day, I was so fired up that I was ready to hang up my Air Force uniform and accept a job offer on the spot. They needed someone to help with public affairs and strategic communication, and given my experience and passion, it seemed like the perfect fit. As I talked to the executive director, I made my interest in joining their staff very clear.

"Well, what do you think about the missionary model?" he asked.

My mind went blank. "I'm not sure I fully understand what you mean," I said. "What's the missionary model?"

He then explained that people who felt God calling them to join the staff were responsible for raising up a team of financial partners who would support them in their work as missionaries. Or put more simply, if I wanted to work there, I'd have to go and ask other people to give me money every month so I could earn a paycheck. In one second, my "passion balloon" popped, and my stomach turned.

"How do you feel about that?" he asked.

There's no way I would ever do that is what immediately came to mind. But I refrained, and with the sweetest smile I could muster, I replied the way any good Christian does in that kind of situation. "I'll have to pray about that."

Moments after leaving their office, I had already justified why there was no way I could be a missionary. First of all, I was much too proud to ever ask people for money. Second, I would be the only Catholic working there. And though everyone had seemed perfectly nice, growing up in the "Bible Belt" I had experienced the misunderstanding and tension between Catholics and Protestants, and I didn't want any part of that. This ministry was clearly not where God was calling me. It couldn't be.

I kept the resources given to me piled in the corner of my bedroom and tried to forget about Military Ministry, but I couldn't get it out of my head. A few days later, I couldn't resist anymore, and I dove into the information. The more I read, the more convicted and interested I became.

The executive director had given a book to me by John Ortberg titled, *If You Want to Walk on Water, You Have to Get Out of the Boat.* He claimed it had been the turning point in him deciding to be a missionary. I held the book in my hands and had the sinking suspicion that reading it would forever change the course of my life. Taking a deep breath, I opened the cover. The entire book is based upon a passage in *Matthew* in which Jesus calls Peter out of the boat during a fierce storm, asking him to walk on water.

> And early in the morning he came walking toward them on the sea. But when the disciples saw him walking on the sea, they were terrified, saying, "It is a ghost!" And they cried out in fear. But immediately, Jesus spoke to them and said, "Take heart, it is I; do not be afraid."
>
> Peter answered him, "Lord, if it is you, command me to come to you on the water." He said, "Come." So Peter got out of the boat, started walking on the water, and came toward Jesus. But when he noticed the strong wind, he became frightened, and beginning to sink, he cried out, "Lord, save me!" Jesus immediately reached out his hand and caught him, saying to him, "You of little faith, why did you doubt?"
>
> When they got into the boat, the wind ceased. And those in the boat worshiped him saying, "Truly you are the son of God." (Matt. 14:25-32)

The author explained that, like Peter, God calls each one of us to get out of boat, to trust Him in the midst of a storm, and to step out in faith to do something that seems scary or impossible. The question is not whether there is a calling on our lives but if we will answer it or let fear hold us back from our true destiny.

There was no doubt in my mind that fear was holding me back from a potential calling to Military Ministry. I feared the loss of comfort and job security if I got out of the military and became a missionary. I feared the loss of approval from my family and friends. I feared joining and being rejected because of my Catholic faith. Above all else, I feared failing. What if I couldn't raise my financial support? What if I took a step of faith and it didn't work out?

The author stated clearly that failing was certainly a possibility, which I didn't find reassuring in the least. He also pointed out that, if I didn't get out of the boat, I would never experience the thrill of walking on water. That, I knew beyond a shadow of doubt, would be much worse.

Personal Reflection & Group Discussion

Have you ever felt God calling you to do something outside of your comfort zone?

What fears did you face, and how did you respond to that call?

18

THE CONFIRMATION

I finished the book and was indeed inspired and challenged. But before I took one step out of the boat, I wanted to be absolutely sure I was hearing God's call correctly. I called the executive director at Military Ministry and asked if there were any opportunities for me to volunteer. There was an upcoming event in Dallas, and they needed some help manning the booth. "If you're willing to work, we'll pay for your plane ticket and hotel room," he offered. I agreed.

A few weeks later, I was in Texas with a few other staff members, handing out resources, answering questions, and talking to countless people about Military Ministry. Everyone seemed truly thrilled to learn more about our resources, except for one woman. She was standing off to the side, staring at our booth with tears in her eyes.

"Ma'am, are you okay?" I asked gently as I approached her.

She nodded, attempting to dry her eyes before she looked at me. "My husband is in the Army, and he's been deployed three of the last five years," she started. "We have four kids, and after his last deployment, he was diagnosed with PTSD."

I nodded, remembering that two-thirds of returning troops struggle with Post Traumatic Stress Disorder on some level.

"He turned to alcohol and became verbally abusive," she continued as fresh tears began to fall. "He completely withdrew from life. He wanted nothing to do with me or the kids..." She closed her eyes and shook her head sadly. "He is not the man that I married."

I could feel her pain and the heaviness weighing on her. "I'm so sorry," I said before adding, "You know... Military Ministry has a book called *The Combat Trauma Healing Manual* that has helped a lot of people with PTSD."

She nodded. "A friend of mine gave us a copy, and my husband and I have been going through it together over the last month. When I saw the logo on your booth, I made the connection, and I just had to come over here and let you know that your ministry and what you are doing is saving my marriage, and it's saving my family."

Her eyes were still red and swollen, but I saw something in them I hadn't seen before. It was *hope*. I asked a fellow staff member to join me in praying for her, and by the time we finished, none of us had dry eyes. We talked for a bit, gave her some more free resources, and hugged goodbye as though we were long-lost friends.

I watched her walk away, still processing the whole encounter. "I know she is going through so much, but what an amazing testimony about your resources! It's so awesome to hear firsthand that they really are making a difference," I remarked to the staff women.

"It is," she agreed. "And we get emails, calls, and letters like that every day from people who credit this ministry with transforming their lives or saving their marriage and family," she said.

Though I was only volunteering with this ministry, I felt proud to be part of something that was having such an incredible impact in the lives of others.

By the time we made it back to the hotel, I was exhausted and in desperate need of a shower. But despite the heat, long hours, and being on my feet all day, I was looking forward to getting up and doing it all again the next day. It reminded me of Acts 21:35:

> In every way I have shown you that by hard work of that sort we must help the weak, and keep in mind the words of the Lord Jesus who himself said, "It is more blessed to give than to receive."

I did feel blessed. And as I fell asleep, I couldn't help but envision all the ways I could help Military Ministry's efforts by becoming a full-time missionary.

I woke up early to go to Mass. As I knelt in the pew, I boldly prayed for God to give me one final confirmation. "Father, if you want me to become a missionary, make it absolutely clear to me today and at this Mass." I sat back, folded my arms, and thought, *Alright, God… Let's see what You've got.*

During the homily, the priest reflected on the life of the apostle, Paul. "Like Paul," he challenged, "we are all called to step out in faith to follow Christ and where He is calling us. To share the gospel far and wide. To be *missionaries* for the Lord."

My mouth fell open. Stepping out in faith? Following where God is calling? Are you kidding me? And not only had the priest actually used the word *missionary*, but I was pretty sure he was looking directly at me when he said it. My body was covered in goosebumps, and I couldn't help but smile as I thought to myself, *Touché, God.*

Personal Reflection & Group Discussion

Do you regularly ask God for clarity and confirmation when making a decision?

How does God speak to you? Through others? The Bible? Music? Quiet time? Nature? Something else?

19

GETTING OUT OF THE BOAT

I returned to Virginia and put in the official separation paperwork to get out of the military. My peers and commander were
convinced I could go on to have a very successful military career and were concerned. "Are you sure you're making the right
decision?" they asked. I told them confidently that I had discovered a passion even greater than serving in the military: serving
the men and women in it. While many didn't fully understand or
agree with my decision, they accepted that it was mine to make.

When I told my family and friends, many of them expressed
similar concerns. I quickly learned that those who care about you
the most are often the ones who will convince you to stay in the
boat instead of encouraging you to take a risk. I knew they meant
well, but I refused to let them sway me.

After applying and completing a formal interview, I was officially accepted on staff. The next step was to attend a 10-day
training in Florida. The only catch was that the travel, hotel, and
training cost about $2,000, and I was required to raise this amount
in order to go. The intent was to filter out those who weren't really
serious about becoming a missionary and also to give prospective
missionaries a foretaste of what would be required of them.

As someone who had never fundraised a penny, $2,000 was
a daunting number. I reached out to my friend, Ryan, for some
encouragement and coaching. He was a former Navy SEAL, a
strong Christian, and one of the most confident people I knew.

When I shared my concerns, Ryan tried to reassure me that calling people and asking for money wasn't that hard, but I wasn't convinced. He must have sensed my fear and doubt because he offered to come over and help me get started.

Ryan showed up at my place the following day with a stack of business cards and his seemingly unshakeable self-assurance. Without hesitation, he grabbed the one on top and dialed the number. I watched in disbelief as he said,

> Hi, Dave. This is Ryan. Listen, I just wanted to call because I am sitting here with my good friend Rachel Sherburne. She is a Captain in the Air Force and feels called to become a full-time missionary with Military Ministry. Before she can do that, she needs to raise some financial support to attend new-staff training. I know you love God and support our military, and I thought you would be interested in hearing more about how you might be able to support her. Do you have a few minutes to talk to her?

My heart beat furiously in my chest. *Please say no... Please say no... Please say no...* I prayed silently. I held my breath for what seemed like an eternity before Ryan finally said, "Ok, great! Here's Rachel." And with that, he handed the phone to me.

I took it with trembling fingers, nervously cleared my throat, opened my mouth, and hoped something intelligent and inspiring would come out. I don't remember what all I said, but somehow, by the end of our conversation, Dave had agreed to give me money. I hung up the phone, completely speechless.

"So?" Ryan asked.

I stared at him for a moment before I could respond. "He's giving me 50 bucks," I managed to say.

"Alright! 50 bucks!" Ryan said, holding up his hand for a high five. I slapped it, still shocked by the whole thing. *What had I said?*

How had that worked? But before I could process anything, Ryan was already dialing the next number.

Each call made my heart race, but after three hours, we had financial commitments for almost $1,000. I couldn't believe it. Not only had my friend spent half his day reaching out to his personal network on my behalf, but people I had never even met were willing to support me financially as I pursued my calling. I remembered a saying I had once heard: "If it's God's will, it's God's bill." That certainly seemed to be the case.

I continued to make calls and send letters, and within two weeks, I had raised the $2,000 needed for the training. I flew to Florida where I learned how to share my calling, ask for money, and stay organized as I began a full-fledged fundraising campaign. The staff told me it took most people 18 to 24 months to raise all the financial support they would need to begin working full-time as a missionary. The problem was that I had less than six months until I would be out of the military and no longer collecting a paycheck. I was going to have to work harder... much harder. So I took their recommended goal to raise $100 in monthly support every week... and tripled it.

Personal Reflection & Group Discussion

How have the opinions or support of others affected your willingness to follow God's call?

In what way is God calling you to "step out of the boat" right now?

20

FACING THE STORM

I was told to start fundraising by first reaching out to my closest friends and family which I did. Though I was nervous every time I dialed a number, I treated "support-raising" like a full-time job, and my efforts paid off. I met my goal and raised $300 in monthly support each week for the first three weeks. When I reported back to Military Ministry, they were very impressed by my progress. Apparently, they had never seen someone get off to such a strong start. My confidence soared, and I felt like I was walking on water.

But all the sudden, the wind started to blow. And before I knew it, I was in the middle of a huge storm—the stock market crash in the fall of 2008.

One by one, the appointments I had set up for that week began to cancel on me. The financial world was in chaos, and many of the people from whom I was asking for money had just lost half of their net worth overnight. I sensed the stress of those who told me, "I'm sorry, Rachel, but I just can't commit to anything financially at this time." Others were convinced I was making a huge mistake. "It's going to be nearly impossible to raise money as a missionary in an economy like this," one coworker warned me. "You should really rethink your decision and stay in the Air Force. At least, you'll have a stable job with a good salary and benefits."

When I made the decision to leave the Air Force and become a missionary, I never factored a horrible economy into my strategy. The situation wasn't looking promising, and I was more than a little concerned. I got down on my knees to pray.

> God, I know You have called me to this ministry and that You're going to provide for me. So, I'm going to trust You and praise You whether I raise $300 this week or absolutely nothing.

Immediately, I felt better. Praying reminded me that God was still in control and that He wasn't at all limited by the changes in the economy.

> All good giving and every perfect gift is from above, coming down from the Father of lights, with whom there is no alteration or shadow caused by change. (Jas. 1:17)

It was Friday at noon, and though I had yet to raise a penny that week, I still had four appointments scheduled for that weekend. I shared my story and passion with two couples and two individuals, and all of them agreed to support me. In fact, one couple gave me double what I had asked for. By Sunday afternoon, God had helped me to raise $625 in monthly support, which was more than twice my weekly goal. And that was in two days during the worst week in U.S. financial history.

I still had a long way to go, but I sensed God was telling me not to worry because He was in control and that, if I followed where He was leading, He would take care of me.

> Seek first the kingdom of God and his righteousness, and all these things will be given you besides. Do not worry about tomorrow; tomorrow will take care of itself. (Matt. 6:33)

I wish I could say that I lived out this verse perfectly from then on, but there were several times when I did worry, got distracted by the storm around me, took my eyes off Jesus, and started to sink. There were about six weeks straight when I didn't raise a single dollar. A few of my ministry partners lost their jobs and had to stop their financial support. Not only was I not meeting my goals and moving forward as planned, I was falling backward.

Doubt began to creep in. I started expecting to hear a "no" when I asked people for financial support, which seemed to be happening more and more. I'm not sure whether my lack of success was a direct result of my lack of faith, but it certainly wasn't helping the situation nor did the fact that I started treating each "no" like a personal rejection.

As I was venting my frustration to a fellow missionary, he interrupted me. "Rachel, do you believe God has called you to Military Ministry?"

"Absolutely," I replied.

"Then God has already prepared the hearts of those who are going to support you. Your job is to pray, believe, and keep making phone calls," he said.

His words were simple enough and revealed to me what I was lacking.

> If you have faith the size of a mustard seed, you will
> say to this mountain, "Move from here to there," and
> it will move. Nothing will be impossible for you.
> (Matt. 17:20)

So, I prayed for God to increase my faith, and with renewed determination, I got back to work.

Personal Reflection & Group Discussion

As you step out of the boat, what challenges are you currently facing or do you anticipate you'll face?

How does faith (or a lack thereof) affect your ability to walk on water?

21

WALKING ON WATER

With a mere seven weeks to finish fundraising before my separation from the Air Force, I redoubled my efforts. I believed that, with God on my side, anything was possible. It was a major undertaking of faith and action, but the day before my last official day at work, I met my goal. In a little over five months, despite a terrible economy, I was 100% supported. When fellow missionaries asked about my secret to success, I told them my philosophy: Ask God to do His part, do yours the best you can, and have faith.

I had planned a month-long road trip to visit friends and family before I reported to work at Military Ministry. Though fully funded, I was encouraged to keep any appointments I had already scheduled on my trip because new missionaries typically have a 30-40 percent attrition rate in financial support in their first two years. Despite their initial apprehension, my family had once again become my biggest cheerleaders. Not only were they supporting me financially, but they were hosting dinners and setting up opportunities for me to meet with potential new donors. The road trip was fun and fruitful as I picked up several new supporters along the way.

The last stop before returning to Virginia was to visit my aunt and uncle and their son in Dallas. They hosted a successful fundraising dessert with their close friends, and I garnered nearly a dozen new ministry partners. It was the last official appointment for the trip, but the next day, my uncle came home with a proposition. "How would you feel about speaking at the end of all of the Masses at our church this weekend?" he asked.

That morning, he told the pastor about the work I would be doing at Military Ministry, and though it wasn't common practice to have parishioners make appeals for outside causes, the pastor agreed to let me speak.

"Now, you only have three minutes," my uncle explained. "Do you think you can keep it that short?"

I wasn't sure how I'd explain everything in such a limited time frame but figured I could think of something. "Sure, I'll just need to make some more copies of my information sheet and response card. How many people go to your church?" I asked.

"25,000," he responded. My jaw dropped. "Don't worry," he said with a laugh. "We'll be there to help you."

I tried to convince my aunt, uncle, and cousin that they didn't need to come to all five Masses, but they were adamant. I acquiesced, knowing that, after the first one, they would realize I had it covered. After all, it might have been a huge church, but because I didn't know anyone, I wasn't expecting a big response.

We set up a table with my handouts in the foyer, and right before the end of the first Mass, the priest invited me to make my brief pitch. I made me way to the podium, smiled warmly to hide my nerves, took a deep breath, and began. "Two years ago, I walked into Mass on a Sunday like this," I began, my voice echoing through the microphone. "Only, I wasn't wearing a dress with heels and a purse. I was in BDUs, combat boots, and I had a 9-millimeter pistol on my hip. And I wasn't safe and secure in Coppell, Texas. I was at the chapel at Camp Victory in the middle of Baghdad, Iraq."

I paused and looked around at the congregation, a sea of faces. Nobody moved, and nobody made a sound. I told them about my experience that first Sunday in Iraq. I shared with them how God had touched my heart and called me to step up and support my brothers and sisters in Christ… how I had started a choir and a small group Bible Study. I told them how, in the end, God had used me as an instrument to lead others closer to Him. I shared how God had sparked my passion for sharing the light of Christ with others, especially with those in the military. Then, after a brief explanation of Military Ministry's support of troops and families, I invited those interested in learning more to meet me in the back of church after Mass.

I concluded by summarizing why I was so passionate about God and the military. "I've heard it said that only two defining forces have ever offered to die for you…" I started. "One is Jesus Christ. The other is the American soldier. One died for your soul. The other died for your freedom. I pray that you'll partner with me, and together, we can serve those who so selflessly serve us." My voice cracked with emotion as I spoke the last few words, and tears welled up in my eyes. I managed a "thank you" before bowing my head and making a beeline for the back of the church.

The applause was strong and loud, but it wasn't until I looked up that I realized the entire congregation had risen to their feet. I felt a thousand eyes on me, and when I finally had the courage to meet them, I saw that many of their eyes were tear-filled like mine. Strangers were smiling and nodding. Others reached for my hand or patted my arm in support as I walked down the long aisle. Only after I had exited the doors to the foyer did the applause die down.

I didn't expect that kind of response, and neither did my aunt and uncle. We quickly dried our eyes and positioned ourselves behind the table as the doors opened and the people began to trickle out. A few folks walked over. And then, a few more. Then, even more. Within a matter of minutes, our table was surrounded. Everywhere I looked, there were people waiting to talk to me, take a flyer, fill out a response card, or place a financial gift in our make-shift donation box. It was unbelievable. And the exact same thing happened at the other four Masses.

Though he was originally not excited about spending his whole weekend at church, when he saw the pile of money, I think my 18-year-old cousin was starting to think the whole missionary thing wasn't a bad gig. When we made it back home Sunday evening, I put him in charge of tallying the checks while I counted the cash. I could gauge the amount of each check by his response. "Cool" was $100 or less, and "sweet" was anything more. When I heard him say, "No way!", I looked up. He flipped the check around so I could read it. I blinked to make sure I was seeing clearly. I had never received a $5,000 donation from anybody... much less, from someone I didn't know.

It took a few hours to sort everything out, but when we finally finished counting it all up, I was amazed. There was more than $15,000 in cash and checks, and more than 200 people had indicated they wanted to support me either financially, through prayer, or both.

I made sure to match the response cards carefully to any corresponding donation so I could write a handwritten thank-you note to each person. But we couldn't seem to find one for the $5,000 gift. Fortunately, there was a phone number on the check, so I made a point to call the next day.

A woman answered, and after introducing myself, I began to thank her profusely for her generosity. "Well, I appreciate your call, but I have to tell you that we weren't the ones who gave you that gift... It was actually our daughter." She explained that they give their children money to tithe each year, allowing them to choose who and what to support. She continued, "Our daughter was really touched by what you said and wanted to support you. When I asked her how much, she said, 'All of it.' Apparently, she has some friends whose parents are in the military, and she knows how much they sacrifice on our behalf."

"Well, please pass along my sincere gratitude to your daughter! What's her name, and how old is she?" I asked.

She replied, "Her name is Brielle, and she's nine."

After we hung up, I sat in stunned silence. The largest gift I had received to date was from a third grader. A third grader! I laughed. Only God. Only God could have orchestrated that. Only God could have even lined up the opportunity for me to speak at all the Masses and moved in the hearts of those who gave. Only God could have raised $15,000 and 200 new ministry partners. And then, it dawned on me. Only God could bring in more money and monthly partners in one day than I had in the previous five months.

> Now to him who is able to accomplish far more than all we ask or imagine, by the power at work within us, to him be glory in the church and in Christ Jesus to all generations, forever and ever. Amen. (Eph. 3:20)

Completely overwhelmed with God's greatness, mercy, and power, I got on my knees to thank Him as tears of joy and gratitude rolled down my cheeks. Seeing the effortless way God provided for me above and beyond what I thought was even possible increased my faith to a whole new level. Not only did God "do something big through me," but through answering His call and stepping out of the boat, I got to share in the most incredible experience I could have imagined... the thrill of walking on water.

Personal Reflection & Group Discussion

When have you seen God show up in an unbelievable way in your life or in the life of someone you know?

What does that reveal about the nature of God? How does that affect your willingness to step out of the boat?

22

DISCOVERING MY INHERENT SIGNIFICANCE

Back in Virginia, I started my new job at Military Ministry with eager anticipation as well as a great sense of responsibility. Before, I was just serving my country; now, I was serving God full-time, too. In a new-and-not-clearly-established role, I had no staff or budget and was responsible for developing, implementing, and growing the media and communication strategy for this international non-profit. As the youngest person on staff, I also didn't want my peers to doubt my ability or dedication. So, I worked tirelessly, despite my increasing stress and fatigue, convinced my efforts were completely noble and selfless.

A few months later at a missionary conference, a speaker challenged my perspective. He talked about how we often base our self-worth on how much money we make, our appearance, others' opinions of us, and how successful we are at work—among other things. He asked us to think about our own lives and to identify things we felt made us valuable or worthy. I knew immediately what it was for me—my job performance and the approval of others. If I accomplished everything on my to-do list and was praised for it, I felt great. But if I didn't or if I was criticized in any way, my spirit was crushed.

The speaker encouraged us to see our true worth through God's eyes instead of feeling validated through earthly, temporal things or even our own efforts. To cement his point, he invited us to spend several minutes in silence to empty our minds, open our hearts, and listen to anything God might want to tell us.

Closing my eyes, I tried to center myself, but I couldn't keep the random thoughts from popping into my mind. I'd try to dismiss them and refocus, but the onslaught was incessant. After five minutes, I was more than a little annoyed.

The speaker came back on stage. "I feel that some of you may need some more time, so let's take a few more minutes," he said. There was hope for me yet. *Alright, Lord. I'm ready and listening,* I told Him. *Anything You want to tell me?* I took a deep breath and closed my eyes. And that's when it happened. It was the clearest and most distinct voice I had ever heard. I couldn't tell if it came through my ears or from inside of me, but I knew with every fiber of my being it was God. *You don't know how much I love you. Why do you try so hard?*

I opened my eyes, half expecting to see Him right there. He wasn't, but as the weight of those words resonated deep within, the tears spilled forth. I knew God loved me, and I could quote John 3:16:

> For God so loved the world that he gave his only Son,
> so that everyone who believes in him might not perish
> but might have eternal life.

But on some level, I still believed that His love was conditional. I lived as though the more I did and the better I performed, the more God would love me. And it wasn't just about impressing God. I was after the approval of the others. I wanted to be valued and esteemed in their eyes as well.

I kept meditating on those words. *You don't know how much I love you. Why do you try so hard?* I felt peace and hope settling in my heart.

Is there anything else you want to tell me? I asked God.

Again, I heard His voice. *Rest in me. I am enough.*

That experience helped me to understand that I don't need to work to earn God's love and grace any more than I need to hustle, perform, or please others to secure my self-worth. The fact that God loves me unconditionally and made me in His image alone makes me inherently significant.

The same is true for you. No matter what you have believed or what people have told you, I pray that you, too, will

> ...have the strength to comprehend with all of the holy ones what is the breadth and length and height and depth, and to know the love of Christ that surpasses knowledge, so that you may be filled with all the fullness of God. (Eph. 3:18-19)

Personal Reflection & Group Discussion

On what false things have you based or are you currently basing your self-worth?

If you really embraced your inherent self-worth and God's unconditional love, how would that change things in your life?

23

LIVING A TRULY SIGNIFICANT LIFE

I used to think that living a significant life meant being famous, making a huge impact on the world, or both. I dreamed of doing something "big" for God and never stopped to consider what that actually meant. Who defines what "big" is? Is it me? Others? Society? Or God? Is it being a well-known speaker and author? Or could it be serving behind the scenes at a non-profit? Is it reaching millions of people? Or could it be impacting just a few?

For years, I had unrealistic expectations, compared myself to others, and questioned my inherent significance. Was I enough? Sure, I had a career, but I wasn't in the C-suite, and I certainly wasn't impacting millions of people. And what about getting married and having a family? Isn't that what every woman is supposed to do? I idolized marriage and motherhood and was surprised to meet several stay-at-home moms who believed making meals, maintaining a household, and raising kids wasn't nearly as significant as giving a presentation in a boardroom, making the sale, or leading a team.

It has taken most of my life, but I now understand that significance is not determined by how many followers you have on social media. It's not based on popularity, fame, your sphere of influence, or any other factor for that matter. You don't have to serve as a missionary, volunteer 50 hours a week, or find the cure for cancer. And you don't have to be a Mother Theresa or a Winston Churchill, either. Sometimes, God calls people to influence the world, and sometimes, He calls them to influence one life. Despite what you may believe, neither is more significant than the other. And that's because living a truly significant life boils down to one thing: becoming fully the person God made *you* to be.

Everything we have—our time, talent, and treasure—is a gift from God. We are but temporary stewards created for a specific, eternal purpose at this exact point in history. In order to fulfill that divine purpose, God asks us to surrender our free will and live out His perfect will which, admittedly, can be scary! It's much easier to go through life following our own plan, feeding our own flesh and ego, and doing what makes us comfortable than taking everything God has given to us, opening our hands and hearts, and truly living out the words, "Not my will, Lord, but Yours."

As much as I would love to understand the big picture, I really have no idea what my life is going to look like next week, next year, or in the next decade. Somehow, I think God wants it that way. If He gave me the strategic plan for my life all at once, I'd likely push Him aside and try to accomplish it in my own strength, feel completely overwhelmed, or question if my life's purpose is really all that significant.

What I do know is that, if I follow God's call, not only will I be on the path to becoming exactly who He created me to be, but He will work through me to bless other people.

As you consider the causes or groups of people you are naturally passionate about, ask God to open doors and to show you how you might be called to get more involved. You don't have to have a lot of time, money, or experience to make a tremendous difference in the lives of others. And if you're like me, when you give of yourself to serve others, you'll be blessed in return.

With that said, you weren't created to be all things to all people or do every seemingly good thing others ask of you. God may call you to volunteer in your community, your church, a civic organization, or in your job as you lead and care for others. Or He may call you to serve quietly at home. He may ask you to say "yes" to something that seems absurd and tell you to say "no" to something that makes total sense. Trust Him, and follow Him. He knows best.

No matter where we are in life, God eventually will ask us to do something that truly requires a huge step of faith. The good and bad news is that we have free will. God is a gentleman, and while His call on our lives is always for our good and the good of others, He won't force us to say "yes" to that call. But I pray you will. If what He has asked of you seems impossible, know that anything is possible with God. And when you hear His voice telling you to get out of the boat, do it! I firmly believe there is no higher calling than the one God has for your life, no purpose to fulfill that will be as rewarding, and no thrill greater than the experience of walking on water.

Personal Reflection & Group Discussion

What would change if your focus every day was to become more fully the person God created you to be?

What do you need to do right now to say "yes" to God's call?

24

Tangible Takeaways

Let go...

Let go of comparing yourself to other people.

Let go of a false sense of significance.

Ask God to show you anything you wrongly believe your significance is based on (e.g. money, job title, possessions, others' opinions of you, etc.) and record those things in your journal.

Below that list, write a statement affirming your inherent significance. Or, rewrite the following:

> Thank you, Lord, that because you made me in Your image and You love me unconditionally, I am inherently significant apart from anything I do or what other people may say or think. Help me to always remember that so I don't look for significance in worldly, temporary things but in You alone.

Let go of anything that is keeping you from answering God's call.

Let go of any fear of failure, selfishness, poor time management, doubt, etc. Record these things in your journal, leaving a few lines between each item. (There's a second part to this exercise coming up.)

Be open to change...

Refer back to your journal and the list you made of your unique passions, skills, and abilities from "Part 2: Hoping in Success."

Pray about **how** you can use your gifts to help other people and organizations, and record these action items in your journal.

Ask God to give you direction about **who** specifically He wants you to serve.

Consider your family, friends, church, community, local schools, clubs, or national outreaches.

Read a book about and/or talk to someone who has fully embraced who God created him/her to be.

What can you learn from that person's courage, authenticity, and willingness to say "yes" to God despite the challenges?

Walk by faith...

Reflect on the following Bible verses.

> Do nothing out of selfishness or out of vainglory; ra-
> ther, humbly regard others as more important than
> yourselves, each looking out not for his own interests,
> but everyone for those of others. (Phil. 2:3-4)

> In every way I have shown you that by hard work of
> the sort we must help the weak, and keep in mind the

words of the Lord Jesus who himself said, "It is more blessed to give than to receive." (Acts 20:35)

For you were called for freedom, brothers. But do not use this freedom as an opportunity for the flesh; rather, serve one another through love. For the whole law is fulfilled in one statement, namely, "You shall love your neighbor as yourself." (Gal. 5:13-14)

Much will be required of the person entrusted with much, and still more will be demanded of the person entrusted with more. (Luke 12:48)

As each one has received a gift, use it to serve one another as good stewards of God's varied grace. Whoever preaches, let it be with the words of God; whoever serves, let it be with the strength that God supplies, so that in all things God may be glorified through Jesus Christ, to whom belong glory and dominion forever and ever. Amen. (1 Pet. 4:10-11)

And the crowds asked him, "What then should we do?" He said to them in reply, "Whoever has two cloaks should share with the person who has none. And whoever has food should do likewise."
(Luke 3:10-11)

Go back to your journal where you listed the things keeping you from following God's call. Use the blank lines below each to write in an applicable verse from above. Ask God to help you live according to these verses.

Write a personal prayer in your journal to commit to faithfully answering God's unique call.

You could also rewrite the following prayer:

> Heavenly Father, You created me with a specific purpose in mind and a plan for me to be part of something bigger than myself. Help me to abandon anything that is keeping me from saying "yes" to You and where You are leading me. I surrender my life to You. Use me in ways I cannot even imagine.

Forgive...

Forgive yourself for the times you have failed to recognize and embrace your inherent significance.

Ask God to help you see yourself through His eyes.

Forgive others whose words or actions have made you feel insignificant.

Considering talking to this person or writing a note of forgiveness that you give to him or her. Or, you could write a note of forgiveness that you simply throw away as a sign you are letting go.

Forgive yourself for the times you failed to say "yes" to God's calling.

If you can answer the call now, do so. If not, let go of the past and trust that He will call again!

Learn to love...

Learn to love yourself and others by intentionally donating your time or expertise to a worthy cause or organization.

Journal about your experience and how it made you feel.

Learn to love God and others by financially supporting a cause or organization you believe in.

Learn to love God and yourself by getting out of the boat and boldly answering His call... no matter what it looks like!

Part 4

HOPING IN AN INCREDIBLE ROMANCE

25

First Kiss

I was in kindergarten when David leaned over and gave me a peck on the cheek. "Ewwww! Stop!" I said, pushing him away. David was sent to timeout for five minutes while I desperately tried to wipe every single one of his "cooties" off my face.

My first *real* kiss happened when I was 12 years old and only because of a dare. Nobody thought I would have the guts to French kiss this boy I was going out with. And by "going out," I mean passing notes and holding hands after school. That was the extent of it. But he was technically my boyfriend, and my reputation was on the line, so I accepted the challenge.

It was Friday afternoon, and there had been a buzz of whispers all day about the kiss that was going to occur after school. I was supposed to meet my boyfriend in the woods by the bus turnaround, so I headed that way. When I showed up, at least 15 of my classmates were already there, gathered around like they were waiting for a show.

My heart sped up. A first kiss is intimidating enough and even more so with an audience. *Play it cool, Rachel,* I silently coached myself. A tiny part of me was excited, a bigger part was curious, and the remaining majority was just plain scared. I knew the main difference between a peck and a French kiss had something to do with the tongue. But I wasn't sure exactly what it was or what I was supposed to do with mine. I hoped my boyfriend did.

I finally spotted him walking toward me with a big smile on his face, and I did my best to offer one in return. He stopped about two feet away from me, and we stared at each other for the longest and most awkward three seconds of my life.

"You still want to do this?" he asked.

I took a deep breath and glanced at my peers circled around us. There was no getting out of this now. "Yep." I lied. And with more confidence than I felt inside, I closed my eyes and leaned in.

I was somewhat prepared for the warmth of his lips but definitely not for the sensation of his tongue in my mouth. My first impulse was to pull back, but I fought the urge, knowing everyone was watching. My classmates began counting out loud, recording the length of our kiss like we were trying to set a new time for the *Guinness Book of World Records*. It took sheer determination for me to stay lip-locked until I heard them say "Twenty!"

Sure, that I had secured my reputation as a fearless French kisser, I quickly broke away, gave my boyfriend a hug, and grabbed my book bag. The boys high-fived and congratulated him on the "longest French kiss ever" while I made a beeline for the bus. The girls chased after me, prying for the juicy details. "How was it? What did it feel like? Did you like it?" they asked me. The real answers to those questions were, *Disgusting!*, *Like a slug in my mouth trying to wrestle my tongue,* and *Heck no!* But to sound cool, I responded casually, "Yeah, it was good."

That seemed to satisfy them temporarily, and luckily, none of them rode the same bus I did. I climbed on board, found a seat away from everyone else, and tried to collect myself. My entire body was shaking, my head was spinning, and I felt sick to my stomach.

I kept replaying the whole thing and analyzing every second of it until I came to the conclusion that not one bit of it had been enjoyable. Wasn't it supposed to be? All the Disney movies I'd seen made the first kiss look like this unbelievably wonderful thing. I expected fireworks, passion, and goosebumps… not nausea. And that's when remorse began to set in. *Why did I do that?* I thought to myself. *I'll never have a first kiss ever again, and that was so bad!*

I kept my face pressed to the window and stealthily caught the tears falling from my eyes. Maybe I was too young. Maybe I wasn't ready to be lip-locking with boys. Or, maybe this particular one just wasn't right for me. But whatever the case, by the time I got home, I had already resolved to break up with him first thing on Monday in case there was the expectation that I would have to kiss him again. There was no way that was going to happen!

I wanted to put the whole experience behind me, but things went from bad to worse when I found out one of the male teachers had seen the whole thing. He pulled me aside after class Monday to lecture me about public displays of affection and how "behavior like that was not appropriate at school or for a 12-year-old girl." I was mortified and so scarred by everything that my next kiss didn't happen for another six years.

Personal Reflection & Group Discussion

What was your first romantic experience like?

How has that or other early experiences affected your view of romantic relationships?

26

LOOKING FOR MR. PERFECT

By the time I was 16 and allowed to date, I was finally over the first-kiss catastrophe and was willing to try again. There were lots of young men who caught my eye, but the good ones were taken, and the rest were either not my type or I wasn't theirs. I had dates to the dances and hung out casually with a few guys, but nothing was ever serious. Toward the end of my senior year, I managed to squeak in one legitimate date that ended with my second real kiss. But apart from that, I was going into college as a romance rookie.

That all changed at LSU. I didn't waste any time making up for all those kiss-less years. But that's where I drew the line. In eighth grade at a "True Love Waits" conference, I made the decision to remain chaste until marriage. At the end of the weekend, my parents presented me with a purity ring to symbolize my commitment. I wore it faithfully on my ring finger, knowing that one day, I would give it to my future husband on our wedding night.

Just because I knew what my convictions were didn't mean everyone else did. I learned that firsthand one night when a guy I had been on several dates with kept trying to take things further. Though I repeatedly moved his hands back to appropriate places, he wasn't giving up. Uncomfortable and unsure of what to do, I made up an excuse about not feeling well and asked him to take me home. Thankfully, he did.

It was my fault for not being more assertive about my boundaries. I should have told that guy what I was and was not comfortable with long before things started to heat up. But I was conflicted. On one hand, I wanted to honor God and my commitment to stay chaste. But on the other hand, I really enjoyed kissing and didn't want to be considered a prude.

When I got back to my dorm, I vented to my roommate about my frustration with the whole dating process and the expectation to hook up and sleep around. "I'm only 19 years old! How the heck am I going to remain a virgin with all this pressure? And if I do, are any guys going to want to date me?"

She tried to assure me that, when I met the right guy, he would respect my boundaries. But I knew that, unless the next guy I dated was *him*, I was going to have to deal with this sort of thing again and again. I could only hope and pray that my "Mr. Perfect" was out there somewhere and that our paths would cross soon.

I first met Andrew on a Catholic mission trip the summer after my freshman year of college. Hundreds of students from all over the Southeast came to Orlando to help repair homes for low-income families. But only one had a LSU hat on, so I decided to introduce myself. It turned out that we had a lot more in common than our alma mater. Andrew was from the same small town my dad was from, our parents had grown up together, and my grandmother had taught him in high school. Conversation was easy between us, and throughout the course of the week, we became fast friends.

Andrew was confident, funny, kind, and radiated a love for God and life that I found extremely attractive. With his dark hair, bluish-green eyes, and athletic build, he wasn't hard on the eyes either. We'd ride the bus together to and from our work site, and it didn't take long for my girlfriends to start peppering me with questions about my "new friend."

On the last night during our worship time, we were invited to find someone else to pray with. I spotted Andrew sitting on the floor and headed straight toward him. Feeling like a nervous school girl, I sat down across from him. He smiled and extended his hands. I placed my hands in his and closed my eyes. As Andrew began to pray, I felt this electric-current pulse from my fingers up my arms and throughout my entire body. The sensation was unlike anything I had ever experienced. He spoke quietly but confidently, and though I tried to pay attention to what he was saying, I couldn't help myself. I peeked open an eye and stole a quick glance. His head was bowed, his face was a picture of peace, and I swear it looked like he was almost glowing. There was a definite physical attraction on my part, but it went way beyond that. I was drawn to Andrew in a way I had never been to any man before.

At the end of the night, I walked over to say goodbye because I wouldn't see him again till we were both back at LSU in the fall. I managed to make intelligent conversation for a few minutes until I couldn't hold back anymore. "Andrew, I have to tell you... When you prayed with me tonight, it was incredible," I said. He smiled shyly. I had never known a guy my age to have such sincerity and serenity, and perhaps, that's what prompted me to ask, "Have you ever thought about being a priest?"

Andrew's eyes grew large momentarily. "Uhhhh... Why did you ask me that?" he questioned. Honestly, I was wondering the same thing myself.

"I guess I just sense this deep spirituality in you," I offered.

He fumbled around with the answer, saying he wasn't really sure, and I quickly changed the subject. After we said goodbye and hugged, I walked away, inwardly chastising myself. *What on Earth possessed you to ask someone who could possibly be Mr. Perfect if he wants to be a celibate, unmarried priest?*

When I got back to LSU for my sophomore year, I pledged a sorority and was soon wrapped up in the Greek life and dating fraternity boys. I still had a crush on Andrew, but we weren't in the same classes or social circles, so I rarely saw him. When I did, he was always perfectly nice and friendly, but he never asked me to hang out or demonstrated any romantic interest in me. So, I set my sights elsewhere. I firmly believed that, if the guy liked me, he'd make the first move. And, if not, I would move on.

I continued to date around, but when I decided to abstain from drinking and partying the next semester to discern God's will for my life, Andrew was the friend who invited me to get more involved with the Catholic Student Center on campus. I started seeing him several times a week, and as my faith was growing stronger, so were my feelings for him. We had built a solid friendship, and I was hoping it would turn into more. Unfortunately, a few months later, Andrew told me he was enrolling in a nearby seminary the next semester. Apparently, when I asked him if he'd ever thought about being a priest the previous summer, he had been feeling God calling him to the religious life and was wrestling with what to do.

I wanted him to be in the center of God's will, so I told him I was happy for him and pushed aside my own feelings. I knew there was no romantic potential, but I needed a date to my sorority formal, so I asked Andrew. Like me, he didn't miss a beat on the dance floor, and we spent the night laughing and cutting the rug. I had never had that much fun with a date, and when we slow danced, I had goosebumps all over my body.

Apparently, our chemistry was obvious because several of my sorority sisters commented on how we made such a great couple. Of course, I knew that was impossible. When I told them Andrew was going to be a priest, they were heartbroken. And even though I reassured them the Catholic Church needed great priests like him, I was, too.

With Andrew off the market, I began seeing other guys. Over the next two years, there were countless first dates but nothing serious. Independent, highly particular, and super involved around campus, I was never the girl who had to have a boyfriend. Casual dating was fun, but once I realized there was no long-term potential with a guy, I ended things.

***

My senior year, I met Tyler. There were 1,000 other R.O.T.C. cadets at this convention in Denver, but the guy on stage with a gavel captivated me. Blonde and skinny, he wasn't my type, but his charisma and take-charge attitude intrigued me as did the jittery feeling I got in my stomach every time I saw him. I didn't know who he was, but I was going to find out.

Thanks to a mutual friend, Tyler and I officially met the last night of the conference. It didn't take long for the conversation to start flowing. We both had similar passions for God, the military, working out, changing the world, and living life to the fullest. He had a handsome face, a great personality, and I became more attracted to him throughout our conversation. We exchanged contact information, and Tyler promised he would stay in touch.

A few days later, I got an email from him, and we began to correspond. With him at Vanderbilt in Nashville and me in Baton Rouge, there was no real potential—that is, until I graduated and came home to Montgomery, Alabama with my parents for a few months before moving to Virginia. It was only a four-hour drive from Nashville to Montgomery, and Tyler asked if he could come see me. I said yes.

Ironically, Tyler had met my parents earlier that year when my dad was the guest speaker for an R.O.T.C. event at Vanderbilt. When I mentioned he was driving down, my parents were happy to have him for dinner. When he arrived, I could tell he was nervous—not that I could blame him. First dates are awkward enough, much less when you add parents into the mix.

During dinner, I mentioned to Tyler that my good friend from college was going to be in Nashville all summer for an internship and that I was hoping to go visit her. "You should totally come!" he encouraged.

I nodded but admitted that my driving and navigation skills weren't awesome and that I had a lot to do to secure a place to live in Virginia and get some furniture before I moved.

"Well, why don't I drive back down next weekend, and I can take you there and back?" he offered.

I thanked Tyler for his offer but told him I couldn't have him driving 16 hours roundtrip for me.

"I love road trips," he insisted. "And I can show you and your friend around town." He seemed sincere and excited, and given my desire to visit my friend and to see him, I accepted.

The next weekend, Tyler drove back down to pick me up, and we headed back to Nashville. With just the two of us, it was a lot more comfortable, and it wasn't long before we were telling stories, laughing, and singing along to our favorite tunes. We met up with my friend, and the three of us spent the whole weekend exploring the city and checking out some of Tyler's favorite spots.

On the ride home, I still didn't have any clue as to what was going on between us… if anything. The guys I dated had always been bold and taken the lead in moving forward romantically. But Tyler wasn't like that. In some ways, he acted more like a brother than a potential boyfriend. I couldn't tell if it was because guys from Oregon were different, he was taking things slowly, or he just had no experience with girls whatsoever.

When we made it back to Montgomery, my parents felt bad that he was going to turn around and drive all the way back. "Tyler, you are welcome to stay here and spend the night in the guestroom," they offered.

He looked at me as if asking for permission. "You should stay," I told him. "But we're going out for dinner," I added. I wanted some time alone with him to see if there was any romantic potential or not.

Dinner was followed by a movie. And the movie was followed by a kiss, a really incredible kiss. There was definitely a spark between us. But while Tyler was clearly past the friend zone, this was not exactly the ideal time for me to get a boyfriend. I would be moving to Virginia in a few weeks to start my Air Force career, and Tyler had a fifth year at Vanderbilt. So that night, I prayed and decided that, despite some amazing chemistry, it would be best for us to remain friends—at least, for the next year.

When I shared my decision with Tyler the next morning, he didn't hide his disappointment. He really wanted to take our relationship further and date me, but I had made up my mind. I could see the hurt on his face as he drove away, but Tyler wasn't one to give up easily. He continued to call regularly after I had moved to Virginia and always managed to stick a postcard or package in the mail to me. His gestures were thoughtful, but they weren't changing my mind. Besides being busy with work, I had a whole lot of "distractions" as a new Air Force lieutenant… in the form of hot fighter pilots.

When my dad found out my first Air Force assignment would be working at a fighter base, he sat me down and warned me about the kind of guys who liked "fast planes, fast cars, and fast women." I assured him that I wasn't a fast woman and that I would stay true to my commitment to save myself for marriage. I knew my purity was the greatest wedding gift I could give my future husband, and I wasn't going to compromise that.

I also knew that, as a 22-year-old virgin, I was an anomaly. While I didn't announce that fact to the whole world, I didn't hide it either. It was nothing to be ashamed of, and the last thing I wanted were guys pursuing me with only one purpose in mind. So, I made sure any guy I dated knew about my standards early on so I didn't waste their time or mine.

At first, I think most of them assumed that I was just putting on a "good girl" act or that, over time, they could wear me down. But after several months, plenty of dates, and nothing more than kissing, they realized I wasn't just talking the talk. And once word traveled around that I really wasn't going to hook up or sleep around, a lot of the guys who were only interested in that moved on.

But despite the "Top Gun" stereotype, not all fighter pilots are cocky womanizers, and I dated some great ones. By that time, I knew I didn't have to sleep with a guy for him to like me and that some actually respected me more because I didn't. On more than a few occasions, they admitted to me how special it was that I was saving myself for marriage and encouraged me to stay the course.

Several girlfriends told me the same thing and confessed that they wished they had saved themselves for marriage. When I asked why they didn't recommit to abstinence, they would shrug their shoulders or act like sex wasn't a big deal after all. But from what I could tell, it was. Few seemed truly fulfilled or secure in their sexual relationships. Then, there were the concerns about birth control, an unplanned pregnancy, getting an STD, or being labeled a "slut" —not to mention the emotional havoc it seemed to wreck in their hearts. When the night or relationship was over, they often felt used, empty, or in need of another guy to numb the pain.

I remembered what the Bible said about the issue.

> Avoid [sexual] immorality. Every other sin a person commits is outside the body, but the immoral person sins against his own body. (1 Cor. 6:18)

His Word is meant to protect us from being hurt physically, emotionally, and spiritually. And while some people tried to tell me that casual sex was all fun and games, I wasn't buying it. I knew I wanted intimacy with a man to be about more than physical gratification. I wanted it to mean something. I wanted it to represent selfless love, a life-long commitment to my husband, and an openness to having children.

I continued to date and remained chaste. It required self-discipline, setting clear boundaries, and making sure I stuck to them. But I was resolute. Not only did it eliminate a lot of unnecessary heartache and drama in my life, but it also allowed me to evaluate a relationship based on who that person was—not just what kind of sexual chemistry we had. I knew that even the most amazing physical attraction and spark wouldn't last forever and that a true,

lifelong relationship had to be built on something much more concrete and substantial: *friendship*.

Personal Reflection & Group Discussion

*What qualities do you find most attractive in someone of the opposite
sex?*

*What sort of boundaries have you established when it comes to physi-
cality in a relationship?*

27

THE INEVITABLE HEARTBREAK

Despite dating some wonderful guys, I could never seem to develop strong feelings for them. After a lot of introspection, I realized why. I was in love with Andrew. I had been for years. When I confessed this to my mom, she asked, "Well, why don't you tell him how you feel?" This was not something I had considered. He had been in seminary for a few years and, in my mind, was off limits. She reminded me that my own grandfather left the seminary after six years to marry my grandmother. "You never know what could happen," she said. "And Andrew's not a priest yet."

The prospect of openly sharing my feelings was both exciting and terrifying. I didn't know how the conversation would go, but I knew one thing for sure: things between us would never be the same again. After several days of prayer, I realized, if I never said anything, I would always wonder, *What if?* And not wanting to have any regrets, I decided to go for it.

Andrew and I usually talked on the phone every few months, so the call wasn't completely out of the blue. I waited till we had caught up for a bit, and then, I took a deep breath and dropped the bomb. I told Andrew how I had liked him for years and, despite trying to date other people, I compared every guy to him. "I know you're in seminary, and maybe you've never thought about me that way, but I just had to call you. If this makes things totally weird and you never want to talk to me again, I'll understand. But at least now, you know how I feel."

I closed my eyes and held the phone to my ear as my heart thundered in my chest. There was no sound on the other end, and with each passing second, my hope crumbled further. I figured he was trying to think of something nice to say to let me down easy. I was seriously contemplating just hanging up the phone when I heard Andrew clear his voice.

"I have feelings for you, too," he said.

Relief and joy swept over my body. Andrew went on to say that, though he felt called to be a priest, he thought about me often. And that, when he contemplated life outside of the seminary, he had even thought about moving to Virginia to see if things would work out between us.

My mind raced as I imagined us together as a couple. I just knew, if we had a chance to date, it would only be a matter of time till we were married. But Andrew made it clear that he wasn't planning on leaving the seminary anytime soon. He was going to follow where God was leading him whether it was to the priesthood or marriage. We agreed to continue talking on the phone occasionally, but dating wasn't an option as long as he was in formation to be a priest. I respected that, and I decided that I would wait for him… however long it took.

Phone calls every few months with a man who was in seminary in Louisiana wasn't the incredible romance I had dreamed of, but I held out hope and continued to wait. Months turned into a year… then, two. He was still in seminary, unsure of his call. I got to see Andrew briefly a few times when I was down South visiting my family. Though, to avoid any perception of impropriety, we either hung out at the seminary, a church, or with my family.

I was growing impatient, but two pivotal events were looming. I was preparing for my deployment to Iraq, and Andrew was preparing for his ordination as a deacon. Once he made these vows—which included a vow of chastity—marriage was no longer an option on the table.

I made one last trip to Louisiana to see him and my family before I left for Baghdad. He came over to hang out, and as always, we had a great time. Andrew and I could cut up and laugh till we cried or talk about the most serious issue for hours, sharing the deepest fears and desires of our hearts as we discussed passions, struggles, God, and His purpose for our lives.

After my family had gone to bed, Andrew and I stayed up talking late into the night. We danced around the issue of "us" several times, but he was still praying about God's will for his life and was picking his words carefully. Part of me wanted to come out and ask him, "Do you see your future being a priest or with me?" But I didn't. In the end, I knew he needed to come to that conclusion on his own and without any pressure from me.

Before he left, we stood and held hands to pray. I felt the warmth and security of his hands holding mine. I listened to the sound of his voice, so deep and sincere as he asked God to protect me spiritually, emotionally, and physically on my upcoming deployment. Being in his presence was relaxing, refreshing, and exhilarating all at the same time. *This is the man I want to spend the rest of my life with,* I thought to myself.

I imagined being in his arms and how easy it would be to lean forward right then and finally kiss the man I loved. *Help me have pure thoughts and self-control,* I silently prayed. And with God's grace and every ounce of my will power, I did.

When Andrew finished praying, his eyes met mine. We held our gaze for several long seconds. *What is he thinking? Is he going to kiss me?* My mind raced faster than my pulse as I waited to see what would happen next. Finally, Andrew leaned forward slowly... and hugged me.

It wasn't what I was hoping for, but I held on good and strong, just like I had those past few years. All the praying, dreaming, and pleading with God for the past two years had only increased my longing for this man. I would go anywhere and do anything if it meant I could marry Andrew.

A few weeks after our visit and days before I left for Baghdad, Andrew called to let me know he had postponed his vows to become a deacon for six more months. I didn't know how much I had played into this decision, and he didn't go into much detail. He just said there were some things he needed to work through and asked for my prayers. As we hung up, I felt a surge of hope that God was answering mine. I would be praying alright, praying that Andrew would finally realize his true calling wasn't to be a priest but to be my husband.

We exchanged many long letters back and forth during my deployment as the anticipation continued to build. His ordination—if it was going to happen—was only a few months away. And finally, a few weeks before I came home, I couldn't take it any longer. I drafted an email to Andrew to see what his plans were for the future and hit send before I could change my mind.

Andrew responded by saying he wanted to wait and talk in person when I got home, but I persisted. Perhaps it was the stress of war and a lack of sleep, but I had waited long enough. A few days later, I got an email from him. His response was quite long, and I scanned through it, desperate to see if my dreams would come true. Instead, I got to the line that crushed them. *While the option of marrying you or becoming a priest are both amazing vocations, I clearly feel the Lord calling me to become a priest.*

I re-read his email, hoping that somehow my eyes had played a trick on me, but they hadn't. I managed to remain composed for the last hour of my shift, but my emotions were bubbling up inside of me. When I was finally able to escape the people and bright lights of the palace where I worked, I began the long walk back to my trailer in the dark. Silent tears watered the ground along the way. Only when I was in the privacy of my small room did the full force of my feelings overwhelm me. I broke down, sobbing uncontrollably from the depths of a broken heart.

"I told You years ago that I only wanted to fall in love once and to the man I was going to marry," I cried out to God with anger and frustration. "Why?" I yelled up at the ceiling. "Why did You let me fall in love with Andrew if, this whole time, You knew he was going to be a priest?" I collapsed onto my bed and wept bitterly. Andrew had been everything I had ever prayed for in a husband and was the only man I had loved. It only made sense to me that, if the love of my life was becoming a priest, I wasn't meant to be married.

I laid on the bed, unsure of how to stop the pain or console myself. "God, help me," I sobbed. And that's when I saw it.

As if in a dream, I noticed the silhouette of a man standing before me. I couldn't see his face because the most magnificent golden light was shining from behind and all around him. He seemed to be coming close to me, and as he approached, I knew it was Jesus. He didn't say anything, but He was holding something. He extended his arm toward me, revealing what it was… a single, absolutely perfect, radiant red rose.

Suddenly, I was no longer crying, and it felt like a warm blanket was covering my entire body. The moment I became aware of my surroundings, the vision was gone. I blinked several times, hoping to recapture what I had just seen, but it was no use. There was nothing between me and the wall of the trailer, but I was sure Jesus had just been standing there. Somewhere within me, I sensed Him say, *I have true love for you.*

Peace supernaturally filled my body, and the ache in my heart dissipated. My eyelids suddenly felt very heavy, and the moment I closed them, I fell asleep. I awoke the next morning, feeling more rested than I had in months. The details of the night were still vivid, and I knew beyond a shadow of a doubt that it wasn't just a dream. Jesus Himself had come to me to ease my pain and comfort me.

> When the just cry out, the Lord hears and rescues them from all distress. The Lord is close to the broken-hearted and saves those whose spirit is crushed. (Psa. 34:18-19)

It amazed me that, with billions of people in the world, the God of the Universe cared enough about me and my broken heart to minister to me in my hour of need. Maybe Andrew didn't love me the way I hoped he would, but it was reassuring to I know God did and that He always would.

> The Lord is with me to the end. Lord, your love endures forever. Never forsake the work of your hands! (Psa. 138:8)

After redeploying back home, I flew to Louisiana to witness Andrew take his vows to become a deacon, and six months later, I attended his ordination and first Mass as a priest. I wanted to be there to support him, but it was like watching the love of my life getting married to someone else. I tried to take comfort in knowing that, if I had to lose the man I loved, at least it was to Jesus. But I still cried my way through both ceremonies.

***

A broken heart doesn't heal overnight, and mine was no different. There were a few guys pursuing me, but I kept them at a distance. One of the most persistent was Tyler.

Tyler had flown to Virginia several times over the years to visit and repeatedly expressed his desire to date me. Because my feelings for him were inconsistent and I was wrapped up in Andrew, I used the long-distance excuse to "just be friends."

That changed when Tyler got an assignment to Langley Air Force Base. He needed to see if there was any relationship potential and knew the only way that was going to happen was if we lived in the same zip code. When he told me the news, I had mixed emotions but not much time to process them. Tyler moved to Virginia three weeks later.

We spent some time together, but after a month and no romantic feelings developing, I finally asked him to meet me for lunch where I told him directly that we would "never be more than just friends." It felt a bit harsh, but I didn't want him holding on to hope like I had with Andrew for all those years, only to have his heart broken in the end. Somewhere out there was a woman who would be head over heels for him, and he deserved nothing less.

Personal Reflection & Group Discussion

Recall a time when you experienced a heartbreak over a relationship. How did you get through the pain?

What did you learn from that experience?

28

STRANGE SIGNS AND UNEXPECTED ATTRACTION

Tyler and I agreed to remain friends, and several months later, I reached out to see if we could catch up. He agreed to meet me for a walk around my neighborhood that warm summer night, just as the sun was setting.

"So, what's been going on?" I asked, hoping to move past any awkwardness between us. Tyler had been traveling a lot for work and admitted that he was dating someone. When I pressed for details, it was clear he wasn't interested in discussing his dating life with me, so I changed the subject. As we swapped stories about our lives in the Air Force, our dreams, and our passions, the tension dissipated. Soon, we were laughing and cutting up.

Hot and sweaty, we decided to run through the neighborhood lawn sprinklers, chasing each other like fools until we were out of breath and soaking wet. I hadn't laughed that hard in months, and as I looked over at Tyler, I felt a slight tug of attraction. *It must be adrenaline or the heat getting to my head,* I thought, dismissingly.

We were about halfway through our three-mile walk when, all of the sudden, the streetlight directly over us suddenly went out. "That's really weird," Tyler said. "When I grew up in Portland, I would go running at night, and I swear the streetlights always seemed to go out as I was running under them."

"Maybe you're just a freak," I offered sarcastically.

"Maybe," he laughed.

As we continued to walk, my attraction to Tyler was increasing, which was both confusing and frustrating. I tried for years to muster romantic desire to no avail and completely shut that door months ago. Where were these feelings coming from?

A few minutes later, there was a lull in the conversation, and we walked in silence for a bit. "Hey," I said with mock seriousness. "Wouldn't it be weird if another streetlight went off?" No sooner had the words come out of my mouth than did the streetlight above us go out. This time, we were both flabbergasted. "Okay, that was definitely weird," I conceded.

"Maybe you're the freak," Tyler suggested with a smile.

I was starting to think the whole streetlight thing was more than a coincidence. *Are you trying to tell me something?* I asked God. I didn't know what to make of my feelings and hoped it wasn't me just wanting what I couldn't have. After all, Tyler had moved on, and so had I.

Looking over at him, I felt a strong pull of desire. It was time to be direct with God. *Alright Lord*, I prayed silently, *if my random attraction and this whole streetlight thing is some kind of sign that Tyler and I are supposed to be together, then make one more streetlight go out as we walk under it.* I was a bit flippant with my prayer, but I meant it. If these feelings were real and God-given, I wanted to know about it. If not, I wanted them to go away.

We were almost back to my house as we walked in silence, passing one streetlight after another. Nothing happened, and there were only a few left. *This is silly*, I thought to myself. *God doesn't talk to people through streetlights.* And that's when the streetlight directly over us suddenly went out.

Tyler and I both stopped in our tracks. When we finally turned and looked at each other, he had the same incredulous look on his face that I'm sure I had. "What are you thinking right now?" I finally asked.

He shook his head and wouldn't answer. "What are you thinking?" he asked.

I shook my head as well. There was no way I was going to tell him about my feelings or my prayer to God.

We arrived at my house and lingered outside my door. "Are you sure you don't want to tell me what you were thinking when that last streetlight went out?" I pried. He shook his head again.

"Maybe some other time," he said with a half-smile.

I gave him a hug goodbye and spent the next hour journaling about the night. *Could Tyler be the one for me after all?*

Over the next five months, Tyler broke up with his girlfriend. With our Air Force travel schedules, we were only able to hang out a few times. Each time, I evaluated my feelings for him, but once again, they were not very strong or consistent. I could only assume I had mistaken some odd streetlight phenomenon as a sign from God. Besides, I wasn't sure marriage was in my future. Given the vision I had of Jesus giving me a red rose, I wondered if maybe God was telling me that He alone would be my one true love. And after dating literally dozens of men with no real potential—besides Andrew, who was a priest—this was not out of the realm of possibility.

Additionally, there was another issue weighing on my mind—my ability to have children. Being athletic, my monthly cycle has been sporadic at best, but after training for and running the Air Force Marathon a few years earlier, it had stopped entirely. At first, my doctor thought it was probably just stress or the fact that I had low body fat. But after four years, he was more than concerned. He ordered extensive tests and did a full work up to determine the problem.

The results indicated that everything was fine on my end, but the doctor couldn't understand why an otherwise healthy young woman wasn't ovulating. He gave me a list of options to consider. "I'm fairly confident that, with the right treatment, we can take care of this problem, and you will be able to conceive children later in life," he assured me. I thought about my medical options for a few seconds but didn't feel peace about any of them.

"I don't know where you stand in your faith," I said, "but I believe that God can do anything. And if I'm supposed to get married and have kids one day, I'm confident that He can heal and restore whatever issue I have with my fertility."

The doctor looked at me blankly. He then stated that I was facing an increasing risk of ovarian cancer the longer I went without ovulating. "Here's a hormone prescription that will help you menstruate regularly," he told me. "I think it's great you have faith in God, but this will help you in the meantime."

A few weeks later, on a short deployment to the Middle East, I went out for a late-night walk and some quiet time by myself. Everything was still and silent. Without any city lights nearby, the sky was illuminated with countless stars. Gazing at the full moon, it dawned on me that, even though I was halfway around the world, I was looking at the same moon I saw in Virginia. It seemed exceptionally large and bright, and staring at it made me feel incredibly connected to God. I closed my eyes, completely in awe of His greatness, vastness, power, and magnitude. It was hard to believe that the same God who created the heavens created me.

> When I see your heavens, the work of your fingers, the moon and the stars that you set in place – What are humans that you are mindful of them, mere mortals that you care for them? (Psa. 8:4-5)

I sensed the presence of God all around me, which caused the hair on my body to stand on end. It was as if His Spirit was enveloping me and filling me with His love. I felt so full and thankful for it that tears of gratitude streamed down my cheeks. And in that instant, I knew I was finally over Andrew. My heart was healed, and it was time to move on.

"God...," I said, looking up into the dark sky. "If you want me to be single my whole life, get married, be a missionary, or maybe even be a nun one day, I'll do it. I'll follow wherever You lead me... no matter what. I just want my life to give You glory."

I returned home from that short deployment, and a few weeks later, Tyler and I made plans to hang out. I had seen him a few weeks earlier, and despite all the streetlight confusion months earlier, I hadn't felt any attraction. It seemed the romantic roller-coaster had finally come to an end. We were just friends. And that's why, when I saw him this time, I was so caught off guard. Something was different... radically different.

From what I could tell, Tyler looked the same, but I was un-believably attracted to him. I said nothing but internally evaluated my feelings, trying to find a logical explanation for why they had changed so dramatically. I hadn't planned for, prayed for, or even hoped for those feelings. In fact, I was completely at peace with the idea that a romantic relationship might not be in my future at all. I just wanted to serve God. And that's when I remembered my recent prayer: "I'll follow wherever You lead me... no matter what. I just want my life to give You glory."

I was reluctant to make any rash judgments, especially con-sidering my sporadic feelings in the past. But it certainly seemed that God was leading me to Tyler. I spent the next two weeks ask-ing God to increase my desire for Tyler if it was His will. And every day, it grew stronger. I found myself thinking of him con-stantly, wanting to spend more time with him. And when we did hang out again, the desire was stronger than ever. I needed a way to tell him about my feelings, and with my birthday coming up, I devised a plan.

Because Tyler couldn't make it to my official birthday cele-bration, I teased that he should prove his cooking skills and have me over for dinner. I didn't think a public restaurant was the best place to pour my heart out to him, and thankfully, he accepted my challenge.

I was going to his house on Saturday, but I had no clue what I was going to say. Andrew was the only guy I had ever shared my feelings with, and considering how that ended, I was a little gun shy. The thought of being rejected by Tyler scared me. *What if he has already completely written me off? What if his feelings for me have changed? What if we try to date and it ends in heartbreak?* I wasn't sure I would be able to handle that again.

Saturday night arrived, and I needed some encouragement, so I called my friend Brittany. "Okay, I'm sort of freaking out," I confessed to her. She knew my past and understood exactly where I was coming from. But she also had strong faith and a different perspective.

"Rachel," she said, "God already knows if Tyler is your future husband or not. Ask Him to guide you this evening. And if you feel a peace about it, don't be afraid to tell him how you feel."

It made perfect sense, and she was right. It was time to stop living in self-protection mode and to trust God. I prayed for peace, direction, and courage and then headed over to Tyler's place.

When I arrived, he was in the kitchen and had pots and pans on every burner. He had gone all out, preparing a gourmet meal that would have rivaled anything from a five-star restaurant. And it wasn't just my taste buds that were delighted. Conversation flowed easily, and as I looked across at Tyler as we ate, I wondered if maybe this would be the man I would sit across from at dinner time for the rest of my life.

We did the dishes, shot basketballs into the miniature hoop hanging from his pantry doors, and turned on old CDs as we danced in his living room and reminisced about the good old days. After a good 45 minutes, my face hurt from laughing, and I finally collapsed on the couch to catch my breath.

I couldn't hear Tyler over the music, so I motioned to him to come over. As he sat on the edge of the sofa by my legs, it seemed like the right time to say something, but I couldn't find the words or the courage. I closed my eyes. *God, I need Your help*, I silently prayed. When I opened them, I noticed my hand was not far from his. I gathered up all my nerve and slowly slid mine closer to his until our fingers touched.

There was a flash of surprise in his eyes as Tyler evaluated my move. He looked at me for several seconds before he began to explore my fingers with his. Neither of us said anything, and I continued to pray for God to guide us. After a few minutes, Tyler leaned toward me, and we kissed... our second one ever, five years after the first.

When our lips parted, we smiled at each other. "Streetlights," I said. The word had come out of my mouth, but it was God who had prompted me to say it. Tyler's eyes grew wide.

"What did you say?"

"Streetlights," I repeated.

Tyler looked absolutely confused. "But I never told you. How did you know?" he asked.

We stayed up talking till the early hours of the morning. Neither one of us could explain the streetlights or how we had both prayed the same prayer, asking God for a sign that night. And I couldn't explain my change of heart and newfound interest in him. But we both agreed that God seemed to have been behind it all.

"Where do we go from here?" Tyler asked.

"How about church together in the morning?" I suggested.

And that's what we did.

Personal Reflection & Group Discussion

Do you (or did you) consult God when making decisions about who to date? If so, how does/did that change things?

How have past hurts or relationships affected your current romantic relationship or willingness to be in one?

29

THE COURTSHIP

Tyler and I began to spend time together and explore a relationship that was more than friendship. Given all our history over the years, it was a little awkward at first, and in the back of my mind, I wondered about my lack of fertility. Was I even called to marriage? What if I couldn't have children?

After about a month of dating, I was heading to Tyler's for a date when I felt compelled to seek clarity from God. On my knees, I prayed, *Father, I really like Tyler, but I want to be obedient to Your will for my life. So, if dating him is not part of the plan, please show me so I can end this immediately. But if it is, please give me confirmation.*

That evening, we had a wonderful time. While there was no red flag to stop dating, there was no concrete sign we were moving in the right direction—that is, until two days later when I unexpectedly got my period. Tears filled my eyes as I remembered my prayer to God asking for confirmation. I had told my closest friends and even my doctor that I believed God could restore my fertility if I was meant to get married and have children. Certainly, after four years and multiple medical tests, this could not be a coincidence. And as for the hormone pills the doctor prescribed? I hadn't taken a single one.

When I finally shared the news with Tyler, he too felt it was a sign from God. We decided to date exclusively, and for the first time in my adult life, I officially had a boyfriend. I wasn't entirely sure what I should be feeling or how I should be acting. I didn't have the head-over-heels feeling with Tyler like I had with Andrew, but considering how that ended, I wasn't putting a lot of stock in feelings anyway. Plus, Tyler had amazing qualities. He was patient, loving, and thoughtful. He respected the importance of faith in my life, my commitment to stay sexually pure until marriage, and he never seemed to tire of planning the most amazing dates. He asked great questions, suggested we do a Bible study together, and always made a point to pray before meals and at the end of our dates. Nearly every day, he would text or call to tell me how much he loved me or how beautiful I was. To say I was treated well would be an understatement. Tyler treated me like a queen.

My single and married girlfriends claimed they had never heard of a man being more affectionate and thoughtful than Tyler. "He clearly adores you," they would tell me. I figured they were right, but deep down, a small part of me couldn't help but wonder if all his displays of affection were truly genuine. Everything he said and did was so perfect; it almost seemed too good to be true. But then, I'd think, *Stop looking for problems, Rachel. You have an amazing guy who is crazy about you! Enjoy it!*

After four months of dating, I was invited to go to Rome as part of my ministry work. It was only for a few days, but I had fun exploring the city and meeting other missionaries from around the world. The last night, I had dinner with two new friends, and we spent the evening learning more about each other. Over several courses of bread, pasta, and pizza, I ended up telling them the story of my heartbreak with Andrew, the vision of the rose, and then all about my relationship with Tyler, the streetlights, and the unexpected sign with my fertility issue.

"So, do you think Tyler's the one for you?" my friend asked.

"I think he might be," I answered.

The next day, I flew home, and Tyler was waiting inside the airport to greet me. He was holding something, but it couldn't be. As he came closer, I realized I hadn't been mistaken. It was a single red rose. Considering my conversation the night before and that I had never told him about the vision of the red rose, I couldn't help but feel that God did have true love for me and also a husband. And his name was Tyler.

A few months later, Tyler and I were in Portland for his sister's wedding. After a wonderful visit and celebration, we had a flight back to Virginia scheduled for 6 a.m. I was still half asleep when we arrived at the airport that August morning and wasn't paying much attention as Tyler was checking us in.

"Here you go," he said, handing me a passport, a map of Rome, and a tri-fold brochure he had designed.

"Wait... What's going on?" I asked as I looked through the brochure. "Are we going to Italy?" I asked, now wide awake.

Tyler smiled coyly. "Yeah."

My jaw dropped, and I stared at him for a few seconds. "Seriously?" I shrieked with excitement.

He nodded again.

"Wait... For how long?" I asked.

"Eight days," he said. "And that's all I'm telling you." One of Tyler's greatest pleasures was surprising me, so despite my many questions, he refused to offer up any more details.

We flew from Portland to Atlanta and then from Atlanta to Rome. We got a rental car and drove to a beautiful hotel nestled in the north-central part of the city. After a quick shower, we were just about to head out for lunch when the front desk called to tell me I had a "package" downstairs. I figured they had dialed the wrong number, but the look on Tyler's face told me it was indeed for me.

We walked downstairs, and the concierge handed me a large envelope. I opened it and pulled out a padlock that was inscribed with our names and the date, a set of keys, and a single slip of paper that read, MILVIO. "Your job is to figure out this clue," Tyler told me.

Thanks to a map and the help of Google, I learned that Ponte Milvio is a famous bridge in Rome where couples make a public symbol of their love by fastening a padlock to one of the lamp-posts on it. Then, they throw the key into the Tiber River below as a gesture of their faithful love that will never be unchained.

We hailed a taxi and headed to the bridge. There were literally thousands of locks covering every lamppost and additional fencing set up to allow more people to participate in the tradition. Given our streetlight experience, we searched until we found one with a tiny bit of room. Tyler bravely climbed up on the side of the bridge, and I snapped pictures as he fastened our lock around the outer rim of the streetlight.

After we tossed our key into the river below, we walked across the street for lunch. We had just finished when the waiter brought the check to Tyler and a sealed envelope to me. This one included three quarters and a clue: ONE FOR A RETURN TRIP TO ROME, TWO FOR A NEW ROMANCE, BUT THROW IN THREE… This referenced the Trevi Fountain, another hot spot for lovers. According to the legend, couples who throw in three coins are destined to be married. So, we headed to the fountain, stood with our backs to it, and tossed the quarters over our left shoulders into the water.

I was busy trying to see where our quarters had landed when Tyler reached out his hand and handed a Monopoly hotel piece to me, letting me know we were headed back to our room. All I wanted to do was collapse on the bed and take a nap, but when I walked in, something was laying on it… a gorgeous one-shouldered fuchsia dress that I instantly recognized. I had tried it on while dress shopping with my Mom and sister a few weeks earlier. "Tyler!" I squealed, feeling more than a little bit like Cinderella.

"Look down," he said. There were no glass slippers, but he had purchased and brought not one but three different pairs of silver heels for me to choose from.

After I got cleaned up, I put on my makeup and my new dress and shoes. When Tyler emerged from the bathroom, he was wearing a three-piece suit. He presented me with the final clue, a piece of paper with this Bible verse:

"AND I SAY TO YOU, YOU ARE PETER, AND UPON THIS
ROCK I WILL BUILD MY CHURCH, AND THE GATES OF THE
NETHERWORLD SHALL NOT PREVAIL AGAINST IT."

—MATTHEW 16:18

This was a verse inscribed inside the walls of the Vatican, so
we hailed a taxi and headed toward St. Peter's Square.

We arrived just as the sun was going down. Most of the tour-
ists had cleared out, and we walked around a bit before Tyler led
me toward a spot in the square where two girls were sitting on
portable stools with a guitar. He asked if he could borrow their
guitar, and they handed it over to him. "Why don't you take our
seats as well?" they asked as they got up and quickly walked
away.

I had no idea at the time that this was actually Tyler's guitar
or that, while on a business trip to Germany months earlier, he
had flown to Rome and spent three days scouting out the city and
planning this scavenger hunt.

We sat down, and Tyler reached behind his stool and pulled
out a large hourglass unlike any I had ever seen. The wooden col-
umns around the hourglass were made in the shape of streetlights, and on either end of the hourglass was an inscription. On
the top was Matthew 18:20: "FOR WHERE TWO OR THREE ARE GATH-
ERED TOGETHER IN MY NAME, THERE AM I IN THE MIDST OF THEM."
And on the bottom, "NEVER SETTLE & LIVE LIFE WITH NO RE-
GRETS."

Tyler explained that the hourglass was specially made and
represented God's perfect timing. As the sand poured out, Tyler
told me there was a lot he could say but that there were only about
ten minutes left remaining and he wouldn't ramble on past then.

He placed the hourglass on the ground next to him and
picked up the guitar. I had never heard him play or sing before,
but apparently, with the help of my brother, Tyler had managed
to learn a few chords. He proceeded to strum a tune and sing to
me while I tried to take it all in. When he finished, he reached into

his pocket and pulled out a piece of paper. It was a list he had made years ago of all the qualities he was praying for in a wife. "Rachel, you have every one of these qualities and so much more," he told me. He looked over to the hourglass, which was about to run out of sand, and then back at me. "Four years ago, you told me that you wanted to be involved in my life though you weren't sure whether that was as a friend, or a girlfriend, or a wife," he said. "Rachel, you've been my friend and my girlfriend. And now, I'd like to ask you a question…"

I sat there almost unable to breathe. "You're probably going to want to stand up for this," he said. I stood up with legs shaking as Tyler got down on one knee. He took my hands and looked me in the eyes. "Rachel Sherburne…" he asked, "Will you marry me?"

Time seemed to stop, and several distinct thoughts went through my mind. *Oh, my God. This is happening. Do I really want to marry Tyler? Why do I feel so uncertain? Say something! There's no time to think. This man flew you to Italy, and if you don't say yes now, you'll ruin it all.*

I nodded and said "yes" as Tyler slid the most gorgeous diamond ring I had ever seen onto my trembling finger. We kissed and then hugged as I tried to wrap my mind around the fact that I was engaged. I should have felt euphoria and joy, but it was tempered by apprehension and curiosity as to why I wasn't more elated.

We spent some time capturing the moment and taking photos before we left St. Peter's Square. Tyler had reservations at a five-star restaurant overlooking Rome. We celebrated with a fabulous dinner, and in between toasts and congratulations from random patrons, I tried to shake the nervous feeling in the pit of my stomach. *It's probably just a combination of jetlag and a healthy dose of fear,* I told myself. *After all, marriage is forever, and this a big step… especially for someone who's never had a boyfriend for more than three months.*

By the time we returned to our hotel room, we were beyond exhausted and slept for 12 hours straight. I woke up and immediately replayed the events of the night before. I was engaged. I looked over at Tyler, hoping for a surge of peace or joy, but the same uncertainty was still there. He was sleeping, so I quietly slipped outside to sit on the balcony, hoping the warmth of the sun would comfort me. I held up my hand and looked at the diamond ring sparkle on my finger. *I guess this is as good as it gets,* I thought. Immediately, I felt guilty. What more could I possibly want? I had a seemingly perfect man who absolutely adored me. Yet, I always assumed that when I got engaged I would feel... different.

We spent the next day in Rome and then drove to San Giovonni Rotundo, the home of my favorite Saint, Padre Pio. We then went to Assisi to visit the birthplace of both St. Francis and St. Clare. Our final destination was a villa in Tuscany where we spent three days exploring nature, relaxing, and enjoying delicious food and wine.

It was the most ridiculously over-the-top romantic proposal I had could have ever dreamed of, but things with Tyler felt a little forced. While surprises were fun in moderation, after a week, I was over them. I was used to knowing what to expect, being in control, and making my own decisions. And I liked it that way. That, coupled with jetlag, the stress of navigating a foreign country, and my unshakable apprehension about our engagement led to tension, a few arguments, and even some tears. Part of me wanted to be honest with Tyler about my feelings and how something between us seemed "off," but after planning such an amazing trip, I couldn't bring myself to do it.

Whether out of genuine desire or sheer necessity, we spent much time of our time in the car praying for a blessed and fruitful marriage. This was of particular concern because I hadn't gotten another period since the one months earlier.

After Tuscany, we returned to Rome to fly back home to the States. I figured the whirlwind trip was finally over, but Tyler had another surprise up his sleeve. My parents had driven 11 hours from Alabama and were there to meet us at the airport. And when we got back to my house, my brother—who was also in the Air Force and stationed in Virginia—was there as well as my sister who had flown in from New Orleans. With my entire immediate family present, we opened a bottle of wine and celebrated our engagement over dinner.

I thought for sure the surprises were finally over, but God had one more in store that even Tyler and I didn't know about. Two weeks later, my period came. It had been six months since my last one and four years since the one before. Apart from getting engaged and praying for God to restore my fertility—which He has completely—there was no medical explanation or logical explanation. To me, it was further evidence that God hears and answers prayers.

> And we have this confidence in him, that if we ask anything according to his will, he hears us. And if we know that he hears us in regard to whatever we ask, we know that what we have asked him for is ours. (1 John 5:14-15)

Personal Reflection & Group Discussion

What sort of feelings do you expect to have in a dating relationship? (e.g. excitement, a desire to spend time with that person, peace, joy, etc.)

Have you ever been in a relationship that made sense on paper but, deep down, just didn't feel quite right? If so, what did you do?

30

A Dose of Reality

Because of all of Tyler's prior preparation, by the time we got back home, most of my close friends, coworkers, and family members already knew about our trip to Italy. Everyone was so happy for us and enthralled with Tyler's proposal that I started getting wrapped up in it, too. Hearing comments like "You guys are the most amazing couple" or "What a storybook romance!" made it easy to dismiss my concerns about our relationship. After all, I had an incredibly handsome and successful fiancé who loved God and me and who was the ultimate romantic. What was I worried about?

We decided to get married in New Orleans because most of my family lives in Louisiana. Coordinating the details of an out-of-state wedding and trying to stick to our budget was a major source of stress, so when Tyler offered to take the lead, I gladly turned over the bulk of the responsibility and decision-making to him.

Though he had been the master of sweeping me off my feet before we got engaged, that started to change. Our romantic dates occurred less and less, and Tyler didn't seem nearly as eager to spend time with me. I would get emotional, hoping that if he saw I was upset, he would change. If I pulled away and made him feel guilty about not spending more time with me, maybe he would want me more or chase after me. Only, my manipulation and pressure tactics weren't working at all. And as our wedding date grew closer and closer, Tyler and I seemed to be drifting apart.

At first, I assumed it was the stress of our jobs coupled with wedding planning, but a month before our wedding, Tyler admitted he was struggling with his feelings for me. I, too, confessed that I was feeling unloved and disconnected. Confusion and fear gripped my heart. What was happening to our fairytale romance?

A new lady was volunteering at Military Ministry as our "prayer coordinator." I didn't even know her name, but I felt God telling me, "Go ask her to pray with you." As soon as we were behind closed doors, I told her that Tyler and I were in a rough spot. Carrie was the perfect confidant. Wise and mature as a Christian wife and mother, she listened, prayed with me, and within 30 minutes, I felt like I had known her for a lifetime.

Even still, I didn't tell her everything that was going on, and I certainly didn't tell other people. How could I explain to everyone who had been so blown away by our engagement story that our relationship was struggling? I prayed fervently and tried to spend quality time with Tyler to rekindle our romance, but a few weeks before the wedding, Tyler brought up his concerns again. This time, he mentioned the prospect of calling it off.

I felt sick to my stomach. I thought about the thousands of dollars we had already invested, the hundreds of invitations that had been sent, and the embarrassment of telling all our friends and family. But more than that, I was convinced that the early confirmations in our relationship were proof we were supposed to get married. I couldn't explain the streetlights, the red rose, or my restored fertility apart from God, and those all pointed to Tyler being the one for me.

Clinging to those signs, I dismissed my own lack of peace and convinced Tyler and myself that God wanted us together. We canceled the meeting we had previously scheduled with our priest to talk about our issues and agreed to move forward with the marriage. Tyler told no one what was going on, and Carrie only knew parts of my side of the story, which were usually focused heavily on my absolute belief that God had confirmed we were to be married. Our intent was to protect our reputation as this "model couple" and not burden other people with our problems, but in doing so, we isolated ourselves from receiving the wise counsel we desperately needed.

Wanting a male perspective, I partially opened up to my Dad though I didn't go into detail and only told him we were having a few challenges and doubts. He reassured me that it was normal for couples to have difficult times in their relationships and didn't seem concerned in the least about Tyler's feelings for me. "When he asked me to marry you, he had tears in his eyes when he told me why he loved you and wanted to spend his life with you," he said. "It's probably just cold feet." I hoped he was right.

I busied myself with final wedding preparations and packing up all my stuff to move into Tyler's place. But a few nights before I was supposed to fly down to Louisiana, I hit the breaking point. Deep down, I knew something wasn't right, and the thought of getting married to someone who I wasn't sure really loved me was terrifying. I played out in my mind what I would say if I drove over and talked to him face to face. I thought about just sending him a text message and telling him, "I can't do this." Shaking, I grabbed my cell phone and began to type a message.

I didn't know what was right or what I was supposed to do. I was staring at my screen, hoping for some sort of direction when a text message popped up on my phone. It was Tyler letting me know that he had finished the slideshow for the wedding and was heading to bed. "I love you, Rachel," he wrote. Blinking through the tears, I felt relief sweep over me. As I reread those words, I thought about the dozens of cards and love letters Tyler had written me, the six years he had pursued me, and all the grandiose ways he had gone above and beyond to court and marry me. How could he do all of that and not be in love with me? I reassured myself that this was just Satan trying to destroy our God-ordained relationship. *Once we get married, everything will be okay,* I told myself.

Personal Reflection & Group Discussion

Have you sought or do you seek wise counsel from others when you are in a romantic relationship?

How has doing so (or not doing so) affected your relationships?

31

THE PROBLEM WITH OUR EXPECTATIONS

rowing up watching romantic movies, I couldn't help but find myself in the characters and imagine myself in the storyline. I could relate to the dorky, insecure girl who never felt good enough, and I cheered her on as she found her inner confidence, transformed, and captured the heart of the handsome, popular guy who was considered way out of her league. I've seen myself as the smart, driven woman who wants to be in control and is fiercely independent, so I wondered if, one day, I too would find a man strong enough to lead me and tender enough to protect my heart and allow me to be vulnerable. And I've empathized and wept with and for the woman who, despite her wonderful qualities, struggled with singleness.

I've watched dozens of those movies, and without trying, I bought into the subtle—or maybe not-so-subtle message—each movie conveys: romance is required for happiness. There's no doubt that we are wired for love and connection. But while having romance can certainly enrich your life, if you believe it is necessary for happiness, you might be tempted to do one of more of the following that will likely hurt you, the other person, or your relationship.

1: Put Pressure on the Person

Falling in love is exhilarating, makes our hearts race, and literally floods our bodies with chemicals that make us feel incredible when we're around that special someone. On this "love high," we put our best foot forward, are enamored with this person's wonderful qualities, and are quick to dismiss or overlook any negative ones that might exist. *How did I find someone so wonderful?* we think.

If you're a typical woman, you tell your closest girlfriends all about this great guy you've met. You try to play it cool with him because getting your hopes up only to have your heart broken is a scary thing, but you're anything but cool on the inside. You've mapped out a potential timeline of how things could progress forward in the next few months if everything continues to go well. You've already considered how well his last name fits with yours. You've envisioned the wedding and possibly even future kids. Will they have his hair color, eye color, and build or yours? And just thinking about him makes you smile.

If you've experienced that and have progressed beyond the first six months or year of dating, you also know that this phase doesn't last forever. At some point, the hormones subside, and the novelty wears off. You know this guy is not perfect and being around him doesn't always make your pulse race and heart melt. The quirky habits you used to think were endearing are sometimes just plain annoying, and you've already identified a few things about him that if they were different would make everything so much better. And this is where it's easy to put pressure on him to change.

We want someone to make us comfortable and to meet our needs. We think that, perhaps with some subtle hints or maybe some direct ultimatums, we can get our way. But if you've ever been on the receiving end of that, you know being forced or asked to change is not enjoyable. And being with someone who expects you to make him or her happy is a lot of pressure. Relationships don't thrive in an environment like that, and many don't survive.

If you are in a relationship right now, are you putting unhealthy or unrealistic expectations on this person to make yourself happy or to meet needs that should be fulfilled by God, yourself, or other friends? And are you clearly communicating your feelings or using nagging, manipulation, or control to try to change the other person?

Remember that nobody can meet all your needs. That doesn't mean you should settle for someone who isn't right for you; we'll discuss that in the next chapter. But for now, decide to stop putting pressure on your significant other to change or be your everything. It's not realistic, fair to that person, or in the best interest of your relationship.

2: Question Your Self-Worth

When we expect romance to make us happy, it's easy to base our self-worth on our relationship status. When we are in a relationship and things are going well, we're happy and we feel good about ourselves. When they are not, we're devastated. And if we don't have that special someone in our life, we may wonder, *What's wrong with me?*, or falsely assume that we are incomplete as a person.

I have watched *The Bachelor* and *The Bachelorette* television shows many times and have seen countless young women crushed when the relationship doesn't work out. They will cry into the camera and say things like "I guess I'm just not good enough" or "if he doesn't love me, I don't think anyone will." I know these women are saying this in a moment of complete anguish, but I want to look them in the eye and say, "Just because one guy... *one* guy... doesn't think you are the right fit for him, in no way does this mean something is wrong with you or that you're not good enough." And being single at 30, 40, or even forever doesn't mean you are any less of an amazing person.

Of course, I understand the longing to find love and share your life with someone. If that's your heart's desire, I pray you do. But, I also hope you know that having a boyfriend or husband will not make you more valuable or whole as a person. And being single does not mean you are less so. God created you in His image, and that means you can be confident and fulfilled regardless of whether you are married, dating, or single because you are a complete, invaluable person in Christ.

3: Keep Searching for Perfection

Besides putting pressure on the relationship and potentially sabotaging your self-worth, believing someone else should fulfill you leads many people to search for perfection in a person or relationship. The problem is that perfection doesn't exist. And if that's your expectation, you'll either be miserable in your relationships, single forever, or spend your life going from relationship to relationship looking for it.

That doesn't mean you should settle for someone who's not right for you or marry the first person you date. But there is a big difference between having high standards and having unrealistic ones. A lot of people today are convinced the grass is greener on the other side of the fence, thinking this other person is so much better than the one they are with currently. So, they jump over the fence to seemingly greener pastures, and perhaps, they are happy… for a while. But at some point, they will realize that this person has flaws, too. And if they aren't mature enough to accept that or are unwilling to put forth the effort to work on the relationship, they'll keep searching for greener pastures, never realizing that the only green pasture is the one they are willing to water and cultivate.

If you have bought into some of these traps, it's never too late to change your attitude and approach. Not only will you feel better about yourself, but you'll be in a great position to have a healthy, loving, and respectful relationship.

32

PRACTICAL STRATEGIES FOR AN INCREDIBLE ROMANCE

While I think most people desire an incredible romance, attracting that special someone and then keeping the spark alive requires time and effort. I can't promise that things will work out in your current relationship or that you'll fall in love in the near future. But, if you are serious about having an incredible romance now or in the future, these six strategies are a great place to start.

1: Flip your focus, and get to work.

Instead of looking at what you want from someone in a romantic relationship, look at what you bring to the table. Is the kind of person you want to spend your life with going to be attracted to you? If not, in what ways can you improve? To help you get started, make a list of all the qualities that you're looking for in your significant other. Apart from gender-specific traits, do you possess these qualities? Be realistic as you evaluate yourself, and identify areas you can work on.

Beware of any "liabilities" or things that may be holding you back; work on these first. Then, focus on upgrading your natural strengths and commit to being the best and healthiest version of yourself physically, emotionally, spiritually, and relationally. If you need to get in shape and lose some weight, join a gym, and make a decision to improve your eating habits. If you have some emotional baggage you need to work through, go to counseling or hire a coach, and if you want to understand more about relationships and communication, take the time to read some books and learn from experts in these fields.

The idea is not to become someone different or to put on a front. It's about being the most authentic and wonderful *you* possible. Doing so will not only give you more confidence, but it will make you more attractive to others.

2: Establish healthy boundaries and stick to them.

When you first start falling for someone, it's easy to get swept up in your feelings and compromise your own morals and standards. But because this can be very damaging to you and cause confusion down the road, it's best to establish healthy boundaries early on.

Simply put, boundaries are clearly communicated limits on what you are and are not okay with. Because you'll be teaching people how to treat you, it's important to teach them well. What makes you feel uncomfortable, unloved, or disrespected? What would negatively affect your relationship? What things are necessary for it to work? Here are a few boundaries I set:

- I will not date anyone that I do not trust.
- I will not have sex or live with someone before marriage.
- I expect the guy to pursue me, and I will not call or ask him out until we are dating regularly.
- I will not tolerate emotional or physical abuse of any kind.
- I will not continue to date someone if I don't see long-term potential.

- I will only date people who respect the importance of faith in my life.

The idea of boundaries may seem old-fashioned in today's culture, but they are critical. Not only can they prevent you from getting hurt unnecessarily, but they also help to foster an environment where a healthy romantic relationship can thrive. The only catch is, once you establish boundaries, you must communicate them to the other person and then live by them. If not, they are useless.

The reality is that you may miss out on some dates and some relationships. But do you really want to spend time with someone who won't put forth the effort to call you or will only date you if you have sex with them? If someone isn't willing to honor you and your boundaries early in the relationship, they probably won't later down the road, and you deserve better than that! So stick to your boundaries and trust that the right person will be more than willing to live up to them.

3: Try new things.

Novelty is one of the reasons why new relationships are so exciting, but even if you have been with someone for many years, you can still share new experiences together. Change up your standard dinner-and-a-movie date by cooking a new recipe or going to a concert or play. Consider taking up a hobby or checking something off your bucket list together. It doesn't have to be expensive or require a lot of time and effort. Just do something you've never done together. Not only will you make a new memory, but you'll deepen your connection and likely even have some fun.

If you are single, trying new things will make you a more well-rounded and interesting person. People will enjoy going on a date with someone who has a variety of hobbies and interests and has more to talk about than his or her job and favorite TV shows. Additionally, when you put yourself out there and try new things, you never know who you'll meet!

4: Edify.

Edifying is one of the most powerful strategies you can employ in a relationship. It's nothing more than instructing through encouragement. This means that, instead of pointing out someone's flaws or telling them how to change and improve, you point out their strengths and praise them for their efforts and what they are doing well. Positive reinforcement really does bring out the best in people, so be intentional and vocal about appreciating and affirming others. When you consistently edify your husband or boyfriend when he opens your car door or does the dishes, there's a good chance he'll continue demonstrating more significant romantic gestures down the road.

If you are unattached, edify other single people you are interested in. It could be as simple as telling someone he or she looks nice or graciously thanking the person who let you go first in line or held the door open for you. We all like being appreciated, so look for the good in people, and compliment them for it. If you are genuine and positive, people will naturally be drawn to you. And that could lead to a conversation, a date, or potentially a relationship!

5: Evaluate.

As you start to invest time and emotional energy in a person or relationship, don't forget to evaluate both. Does he or she treat you well, respect your boundaries, and bring out the best in you? Are your personalities, passions, life goals, views of marriage, plans for children, and faith in God compatible? If not, which ones are you willing to compromise on, and which are non-negotiable? These things can become huge sticking points in the future, so it's best to address these issues early on.

You must also evaluate yourself. Are you healthy emotionally, physically, and spiritually? Is this a good time for you to be in a relationship, or should you be single for a while? Is there mutual attraction and interest, or is it mostly one-sided? And is this someone you could potentially marry, or is this more of a temporary distraction or rebound relationship?

Answer these questions honestly, and avoid comparing your relationship to anybody else's or what you see on TV or in the movies. If physical attraction, exotic dates, and fancy food and wine were the only requirements for a fabulous relationship, every contestant on *The Bachelor* or *The Bachelorette* would be in a happy and thriving one. The truth is that the vast majority are not. Romantic gestures and sex appeal are nice, but they aren't the foundation of a fulfilling or lasting relationship.

Far too many people have spent years of their lives in relationships with people they knew, early on, they didn't have a future with. This isn't fair to you or the other person, so if you feel that way, it's time to end the relationship. Of course, your feelings could change down the road, but in the meantime, you are both free to move forward and meet the right person.

6: Seek wise counsel.

When you are in a dating relationship that is getting more serious, it's important to introduce that person to your close friends and people who know you well and want the best for you. God never intended for us to date in an exclusive vacuum, and spending time with those people allows them to see how you interact with this person and alert you to any red flags you may have missed. You don't need to discuss every detail of your relationship with everyone, but there should be a few, wise people you can talk with honestly who will provide godly counsel. And when they do, truly listen to them, especially if they have concerns. We all have blind spots, and while their opinions may not be what you want to hear, they may be what you need to hear. God put us in community for a reason, so take advantage of it, whether you are single, in a committed relationship, or married.

I'm convinced that, if you will live by these six strategies, you'll be positioning yourself for an incredible romance now and in the future. With that said, regardless of your current relationship status, there's still hope. You were made to be pursued, adored, loved, and delighted in, and you can have that right now. You just have to know where to find it.

Personal Reflection & Group Discussion

Have you fallen into any traps that might be negatively affecting your current relationship or ability to be in one?

What practical strategies can you employ now to improve your current romantic relationship or position yourself for one in the future?

33

AN EVEN BETTER ROMANCE

The traditional view of romance is about the love, passion, and intimacy between a man and a woman. And while that is a beautiful thing, it's just a shadow of a much greater romance that we were all created to experience.

As I look back on my life, I can see that I have been romanced as long as I can remember. My Pursuer thinks I'm wonderful despite my mistakes and even when I'm at my worst. He sees me as beautiful, and it goes way beyond what I look like on the outside. He's been faithful to me without fail, and I can trust Him with anything. He's a fabulous listener and always knows exactly what to say. He's a creator, miracle-worker, redeemer, and savior, but He knows and cares about every detail of my life. He's the one my soul was designed to long for... and it does.

I always knew about Jesus, but it wasn't until college that I got to know Him personally and realized He was the real deal and that I could trust Him completely. The more time I spent just talking, listening, and being in His presence, the more our friendship blossomed into an intimate relationship... one that means more to me than I can express.

When I was under the influence of a lie and thought I wasn't good enough, God continually whispered to me, "You are so beautiful. You are perfect just as you are." When my heart was broken over Andrew, Jesus appeared to me in a vision and reassured me of His true love for me. When I was trying to raise my support as a missionary, He provided for all my financial needs above and beyond what I even thought was possible. And when I doubted my self-worth and believed I had to perform and try to earn God's affection, He reminded me, "You don't know how much I love you. Why do you try so hard?"

Jesus has been with me every step of the way and has filled my heart to overflowing in a way that no man ever has or ever could. He comforted me when I was broken, gave peace to me when I was afraid, provided for my needs, awed me with His creation, and showered me with His love—His perfect, unconditional, unending love. And that same love Jesus has for me He has for you, too.

Take the most over-the-top feeling you've ever had for another human being, and multiply that by a trillion. God has more love for you than that. Imagine the most incredible romance novel or movie ever created. It doesn't hold a candle to Jesus' love story. His love is much more than letting you pick the restaurant or control the television remote. It goes beyond buying flowers for you or taking you on a nice vacation. He isn't content with loving you and blessing you in this life. He loved you enough to die for you so you could spend eternity with Him.

> In this is love: not that we have loved God, but that he
> loved us and sent his Son as expiation for our sins.
> (1 John 4:10)

Regardless of where you are or where you've been, God loves you unconditionally and wants to have a personal relationship with you. It doesn't matter if you grew up going to church, have never set foot in one, are a devout Christian, or doubt God exists. Even if you reject Him or curse His name, He will still lovingly call yours, wanting nothing more than to fill every empty place inside of you. And He's the only one who truly can and ever will.

If you want to experience true, eternal, unfailing love in every fiber of your being, a relationship with Jesus is the answer. If you don't know where to start, consider saying this simple prayer: "Lord, I need you. Take control of my life. Forgive me for my sins, and help me to know You and follow You." Of course, that's only the first step. Like any relationship, developing an intimate one takes time and intentionality, but it is more than worth it. I'm convinced that, if you will open your heart and allow God to capture it and fill it with His love, you will discover that the most incredible romance in this life and the next is with Him.

Personal Reflection & Group Discussion

Can you recall a time or experience when you sensed God pursuing you?

How would your life change if you invested as much time in your relationship with God as you do with your best friend or significant other?

34

TANGIBLE TAKEAWAYS

Let Go

Let go of thinking that your romantic relationship should model what you have seen in movies or read about in novels.

Let go of thinking that you have to be in a romantic relationship to be happy.

Let go of sexual intimacy outside of marriage.

Chastity is a beautiful thing and is part of God's plan to protect us emotionally, spiritually, and physically. It also prepares us to enjoy fully the life-giving act of love we will share with our husband or wife one day.

Let go of putting pressure on someone else to be your *everything*.

Journal about any unrealistic expectations you have, and ask God to show you who should be meeting those needs (e.g. God, other friends, yourself, etc.).

Be Open to Change

Make a list of all the non-gender-specific qualities you want in a future spouse.

Next, journal about ways you can work on embodying those traits yourself. Consider asking a friend to hold you accountable, or seek help from a professional.

Try new things.

Do some research and commit to doing something you've never done before to spice up your romantic life or potentially meet someone new.

Prayerfully evaluate your current dating relationship.

Consider your feelings, faith, future potential, friendship factor, etc. concerning your current relationship. Ask God for clarity and discernment, and if you sense it's not the right person or the right timing, don't be afraid to end that relationship.

Walk by Faith

Reflect on the following Bible verses.

> I urge you therefore, brothers, by the mercies of God, to offer your bodies as a living sacrifice, holy and pleasing to God, your spiritual worship. Do not conform yourselves to this age but be transformed by the renewal of your mind, that you may discern what is the will of God, what is good and pleasing and perfect. (Rom. 12:1-2)

The Lord is with me to the end. Lord, your love endures forever. Never forsake the work of your hands! (Psa. 138:8)

I adjure you, daughters of Jerusalem, by the gazelles and hinds of the field, Do not arouse, do not stir up love, before its own time. (Song. 8:4)

This is the will of God, your holiness: that you refrain from immorality, that each of you know how to acquire a wife for himself in holiness and honor, not in lustful passion as do the Gentiles who do not know God; not to take advantage of or exploit a brother in this manner, for the Lord is an avenger in all of these things, as we told you before and solemnly affirmed. For God did not call us to impurity but to holiness. Therefore whoever disregards this, disregards not a human being but God, who [also] gives his Holy Spirit to you. (1 Thess. 4:3-8)

Do to others whatever you would have them do to you. (Matt. 7:12)

Pray about what is important to God and yourself in a relationship.

Journal about the healthy boundaries you are going to establish regarding your romantic relationships.

Write a personal prayer in your journal about your desire to embrace truly the divine romance with God.

Or, you can re-write the following prayer:

Heavenly Father, thank You for loving me, pursuing me, and delighting in me. Help me to value my relationship with You above all else. Draw me ever closer to You, and completely fill my heart with Your love so I won't be dependent on others to fill me or make me feel worthy.

Forgive

Forgive yourself for the times you have engaged in sexual immorality and not honored God or others in your relationships.

If you need to ask for forgiveness from others, do that.

Forgive others who have not treated you with the honor and respect you deserve.

Write a note forgiving this person in your journal, and ask God to help you let go of any residual hurt.

Forgive God if you are upset over a failed relationship or your singleness.

Openly share your feelings with God in your journal, asking Him to heal your heart and give to you His perspective.

Learn to Love

Learn to love yourself and God by inviting Him into the dating process.

Live by what He says in the Bible, and stick to the boundaries you have established to foster a healthy and holy romantic relationship now and in the future.

Learn to love God by setting aside time daily or weekly to cultivate that relationship.

Consider prayer, going to church, journaling, or going somewhere to enjoy nature and God's presence.

Learn to love others by being an encouragement to the brokenhearted or lonely.

Consider reaching out to someone who is single or just went through a breakup. Invite that person to dinner or coffee. Just be willing to listen.

Part 5

HOPING IN WEDDED BLISS

35

THE WEDDING AND
HONEYMOON PHASE

Tyler and I got married in the French Quarter and enjoyed a beautiful wedding and reception with our closest friends and family. A horse-drawn carriage took us to our rustic hotel where we spent our first night as a married couple. True to my plan, I gave Tyler the purity ring I had been saving for the last 14 years. Early the next morning, we left for our week-long honeymoon in Mexico.

Considering the rough spot we had been in before getting married, by the time we said our vows, I was ready to put that behind us and enjoy wedded bliss. I was determined to be the perfect wife, which meant working a full-time job, keeping an immaculate, fabulously decorated house, cooking delicious meals, and satisfying all of Tyler's physical and emotional needs. All my self-imposed pressure made it hard to live in the moment and enjoy life, not to mention that the first year was an absolute whirlwind.

In addition to adjusting to married life and both of us taking on new roles at work that required extensive travel, four months into our marriage, a pipe burst in our upstairs bathroom and flooded our entire house. For the next three months, we lived in a construction zone. There were gutted walls and ceilings with wires hanging out and piles of furniture and decorations everywhere. With the drying fans and constant rotation of contractors working on the house, there was no quiet and no alone time.

After much frustration, we had the house back to normal, and I was ready to enjoy what was left of our "honeymoon year." Unfortunately, a few months later, I came down with mono. Worse than my swollen neck and sore throat was the debilitating fatigue. For the next eight weeks, it was all I could do to walk up the stairs without feeling faint. I lost my appetite and energy and spent much of my time in bed.

Just as I was starting to feel better, Tyler faced a huge setback in his career. He had been hired to fly for the Air National Guard in Alaska, and we had plans to move to Oklahoma for pilot training. He was thrilled at the opportunity to achieve his life-long dream and was at his office farewell luncheon when he got a call that something was wrong with his paperwork. In the days and weeks to come, we learned that, due to a mix up that was no fault of his own, Tyler would not be able to attend pilot training after all.

All of the sudden, our future plans were completely up in the air. I tried to rally around and support him, but Tyler seemed to withdraw and become more and more distant. When I asked him what was wrong or what I could do to help, he said "nothing" or that he was "just tired or busy." Given everything we had been going through at work and at home, I wanted to believe him. But deep down, I knew something wasn't right. And it hadn't been for a long time.

To others, we were a model couple. We looked great together and were successful, highly involved at church, growing our own business, and serving the community. But all the activity was masking the fact that we really weren't communicating, connecting, or spending quality time together. When we weren't doing things, we were putting up walls, shutting down, or pretending everything was okay.

I felt like a trophy Tyler had worked so hard to win but no longer valued. He seemed to prioritize everyone and everything else over me, and I felt neglected and lonely. We shared a last name, a home, and a bed; but often, it felt like we were oceans apart. I didn't want to nag or have to ask him to love me, but there were several times when I broke down and told him how empty I felt. I hoped sharing my heart would motivate him to change, but he would just hug me while I cried and say he was sorry.

Personal Reflection & Group Discussion

What sort of expectations do you place on yourself in a marriage?

What do you or will you need from your spouse to feel loved and valued?

36

THE STORM ROLLS IN

There were no fights or raised voices—just an unsettled feeling like the calm before the storm. But the pressure was building, and 14 months into our marriage, the storm rolled in—literally. We were preparing our house and getting ready to hunker down for a hurricane when we got into a minor disagreement that quickly escalated. Just as the wind picked up and the rain started to fall, Tyler finally confessed his true feelings.

"I don't think we should have gotten married," he said. My heart dropped and then began pounding like a hammer in my chest. He paused and looked pained as he continued. "I don't know how to say this, but I don't think I was ever in love with you." He looked at me, waiting for a response, but I couldn't say anything. "I feel like I'm living a lie... and I'm not happy."

Admittedly, things were not good between us, but I couldn't understand how, given everything he did to pursue me, Tyler could say he never loved me. I asked him if there was another woman, but he said no. When I tried to get clarity and ask more questions, all Tyler kept coming back to was his lack of feelings for me and how he felt like marrying me was a mistake.

At a loss for what else to say or do, I went upstairs and cried alone on our bed as the wind howled outside. I kept replaying Tyler's words and analyzing our entire relationship. *Had he ever loved me? What did I do wrong? What could I do better? Would our marriage make it?* I jumped from thought to thought until my body finally succumbed to sleep in the early hours of the morning.

Tyler slept downstairs, and when I woke up, I called my friend Carrie. Sobbing, I told her the events of the night before. She prayed with me and encouraged me to just spend the rest of the weekend with Tyler without trying to fix everything or even talk about it. The prayers and a shower helped, and when I came downstairs, Tyler hugged me. Because we were stuck in the house riding out the storm, he was relieved when I suggested we hang out and not try to solve our marital problems. We watched movies, ate pizza, laughed, and actually had a pretty good time. Things seemed better than they had been in a long time.

The hurricane came and went with little collateral damage, and I prayed that the storm in our marriage would do the same. I hoped Tyler had just spoken rashly in the heat of the moment and didn't really mean what he had said—or if he had been honest about how he felt about me, his feelings would change quickly.

Over the next several days, I went above and beyond to cater to all of Tyler's needs and wants. I tried to be as fun, sexy, and loving as possible. But a week later when I asked if things were better between us, the answer was "no." I was crushed. I had done everything I could think of. "What am I doing wrong? How can I make you happier?" I asked. He couldn't give me an answer, and I was left trying to guess what the problem was and was clueless about how to fix it.

A few weeks later while at work, I received a random email from someone I didn't know that filled in the missing piece. There was another woman in the picture, and their relationship was serious. In a matter of seconds, my world turned upside down. *This can't be my life,* I thought to myself. Never in a million years did I imagine dealing with marital infidelity, and I felt woefully unprepared to face the storm I was now fully engulfed in. So, I did the easiest and most natural thing; I let my human emotions take over.

Once the initial shock wore off, the emotion that surfaced was anger. I had never experienced such pain and betrayal, and I wanted Tyler to get a taste of the same. I thought about forwarding the email to his closest friends to expose his infidelity. I thought about calling his Air Force commander to expose the affair Tyler was having with this coworker and get them both in serious trouble.

Once my emotions settled a bit, I realized those were both terrible ideas. Neither would take away my pain, and trying to hurt Tyler would only make me feel worse. I wasn't a malicious person, but I was angry—and not just toward Tyler either. I was angry at God for allowing me and, I felt, *calling* me to marry someone who would do this to me. I was angry at myself for not trusting my own intuition and lack of peace along the way. And I was angry that I even had to deal with such a mess. Bad things weren't supposed to happen to good people. I was a good person with high hopes and dreams for my future, and none of this was part of my fairytale.

I soon learned the anger was just the surface-level emotion covering an ocean of hurt. The waves of insecurity, embarrassment, and betrayal began crashing over me. *What was wrong with me? What would other people think? Could Tyler ever really love me? And if he did, could I ever trust him again?*

Every hour was excruciating and seemed to drag on for days. I would have paid any amount of money to simply fast-forward time to escape the pain and rejection I felt in every fiber of my being. I went on a walk to clear my head and talk to God. *Why did this happen?* I asked. I was searching for an answer but heard only the wind in my ears. *Ok, well, how am I supposed to get through this?*

I felt God speak to my spirit, "Stay the course."

"But God," I argued, "Tyler said he doesn't even think we should have gotten married. What if this whole thing is a big mistake?"

Deep within, I sensed Him speak. "I do not make mistakes."

Immediately, I thought back to the many ways God had gone above and beyond to confirm my relationship with Tyler. He had a point. "Okay," I conceded, "But my heart is so broken. How am I supposed to live through this agony?"

I was hoping God would say, "I'm to going to change Tyler's heart right now." Or, at least, "I'm going to take away all of your suffering." But those answers didn't come. The advice was simple: "Rest in me."

I looked up and noticed the sun was peeking through the overcast sky. I stopped, breathed deeply, and allowed the warmth of its rays to comfort me. I thought about what God told me: *Stay the course. I do not make mistakes. Rest in me.* It sounded pretty straightforward, but I would soon discover that believing in and living by those simple statements would be much more difficult than I expected.

Personal Reflection & Group Discussion

Have you ever faced betrayal in a relationship? If so, how did that feel?

What is your initial response when someone hurts you?

37

STRIVING FOR CONTROL AND TRYING TO SURVIVE

I might not have been able to speed up time, but I was interested in doing whatever I could to speed up the restoration process. I started with Tyler and told him in no uncertain terms what he needed to do: "End it with this other woman, and go to counseling with me." I also reached out to his two best friends, hoping they could talk some sense into him. If Tyler wouldn't listen to me, I hoped he would listen to them.

Next, I set my sights myself. Because Tyler had cheated on me with another woman, I could only assume that, somehow, I wasn't good enough. I experimented with trying to modify my personality, behavior, and appearance, hoping to reclaim Tyler's heart and win him over. I also bought a dozen self-help books on relationships and went online to research "how to save a broken marriage." If there was a solution out there to redeem ours, I was going to find it.

Finally, I turned to God and asked Him to save our marriage. I assumed—if I did enough praying, Bible reading, and fasting— God would honor my efforts and restore our marriage quickly. One day, while praying along those lines, I felt Him say, *Don't rush this time. You don't know what I am doing.* I sat back dumbfounded. I sure didn't. What was He doing after all? Nothing was changing.

I had never worked so hard for anything in my life. And I had never gotten such poor results. Not only was it exhausting, but it seemed the harder I tried to control things the worse they got. And Tyler confirmed that a few weeks later when he told me his feelings hadn't changed at all.

Beyond frustrated, I stomped upstairs and slammed the bedroom door as hot, angry tears spilled forth. "This is hopeless!" I cried to God. And a large part of me hoped it was. I wanted nothing more than to pack my bags, load up my car, and drive far away from my house, my broken marriage, and my unfaithful and unloving husband.

I grabbed my Bible and told God in no uncertain terms that I needed some sort of sign that this marriage was even worth fighting for. I randomly opened my Bible and landed on a page in the book of *Jeremiah*. I had underlined a verse on each page sometime before, and my eyes were drawn there. The first was Jeremiah 32:17:

Ah, my Lord God! You made the heavens and the earth with your great power and your outstretched arm; nothing is impossible for you.

On the next page, verse 27 was underlined.

I am the Lord, the God of all the living! Is anything impossible to me?

Goosebumps covered my body. I sensed God was telling me not to give up or lose hope no matter what Tyler said or what things looked like. He was, after all, the God of the impossible, and He could do anything—even redeem what seemed to be a lifeless and hopeless marriage.

While those verses reassured me, the God of the impossible didn't swoop in and rescue me or redeem my marriage that night, the next night, or the one after that. Although I was willing to move forward and work on our marriage, Tyler wasn't. We attempted a few counseling sessions, but because he was convinced marrying me was a mistake, it was pointless. On our 18-month anniversary, he told me he was moving out. The next day, the day before Thanksgiving, Tyler packed up some of his stuff and went to stay with a friend from work.

The first night he was gone, I managed to hold it together. *He'll be gone for a few days, but when he realizes how much he really does love and miss me, he'll come back.* At least, that's what I told myself as I pulled out the Christmas boxes and started decorating the house. It was a temporary distraction, but as the days turned into weeks, it got much harder.

I didn't know how to live this separated life or what to tell people. I was embarrassed and didn't want everyone to know about our marital problems—especially because I hoped they would be resolved quickly. But that left me with either trying to keep my distance from others or having to pretend that everything was "just great" when I was around them. I'm not sure what was worse—feeling isolated and alone or feeling like I was living a lie. I knew I didn't need to broadcast all the details of my personal life to everybody—certainly not over social media. But I also knew I needed the support of others, so I finally reached out to those closest to me.

My parents and immediate family were understandably quite upset when they heard the news. They offered to fly me home for a while, but I declined. Even if I could temporarily escape my marriage problem, it would be there when I returned. Plus, being surrounded at work by amazing Christian women who could encourage and pray for me regularly was what I needed more than anything.

Tyler moving out was a major setback, but I was determined to save our marriage. I continued to spend time with him when possible, and I'd analyze our every interaction. If he asked me to hang out or told me I was pretty, I'd assume his desire for me was increasing. And every hug or kiss had me hoping we were one step closer to reconciliation.

But Tyler's actions and words weren't consistent. I kept looking at him, waiting for things to change, but we weren't moving toward divorce or reconciliation. He didn't care enough to fight for me or let me go. His apathetic response was emotional torture, and after several months, I was on the verge of a breakdown.

I called my friend Carrie in tears. "I knew you were going to call," she said matter-of-factly. "The Lord literally gave me a word for you two minutes ago." She continued, "God told me, 'Rachel is looking at Tyler and not at me, and that's why this is so hard. She has to keep her eyes fixed on Me.'"

The truth was that my eyes were glued on Tyler. Carrie's words reminded me of the story of Peter walking on water. As long as my eyes were locked on Jesus, I was okay, but the minute I looked at Tyler and the stormy waters of our broken marriage, I found myself drowning in a sea of despair.

Personal Reflection & Group Discussion

When facing a painful situation or storm in life, do you ask God for guidance?

How have friends and family supported you during difficult times?

38

UNDER ATTACK

Though I wanted to keep my eyes fixed on Christ, it seemed at my weakest moments, Satan was right there to distract or tempt me. It usually came in the form of an attractive man at the gym who would pay me a compliment or the guy who would smile and say hello as he passed me in the grocery store. I wore my wedding ring every single day, but there were plenty willing to overlook that and a few bold enough to ask me out on dates. I knew to accept any such offer would be playing with fire. None of my needs were being met by Tyler, and I was in a vulnerable place. And that's when the biggest temptation came.

It was shortly after my 30th birthday that an old fighter pilot friend from my past popped up on Facebook. I hadn't talked to him in years, but we had dated briefly and had lots of chemistry. When I read the very suggestive message he sent me, desire and longing swept over me. Tyler wasn't meeting any of my physical or emotional needs, but I was sure this guy would.

I imagined meeting up for coffee or maybe getting lunch. And what started as fairly innocent scenarios rapidly turned into lustful ones. I felt ashamed that I was a Christian missionary fantasizing about having an affair with a married man. But being a Christian or a missionary didn't make me immune from temptations or the desire to act upon them.

I arrived at work the next morning, hoping a good dose of prayer and Bible study would give me some clarity. As I looked around at my fellow coworkers, I realized they knew nothing of my internal battle and also that Satan wanted to keep it that way. Maybe I was strong enough to resist his bait now, but what about in a few days or weeks when I was alone or feeling empty? I was sure his attack would continue, and that fact alone made me resolute about what I needed to do.

After a devotional time, I grabbed one of my best friends at work and pulled her into my office. I'd known Frances for years, and she knew about this guy from my past. As I told her everything that had transpired, she could see I was struggling and didn't mince words. "You know what you need to do," she said. "Absolutely nothing good can come from this." I nodded soberly. "You don't even want him," she reminded me. "You just want what he can give you... attention and the feeling of being wanted." That was also true. "And," she continued, "if you go down this road, not only will you regret it in the long run, but your marriage won't be able to survive this. You'll compare this guy to Tyler, and after everything he's done to hurt you, Tyler won't measure up."

I knew she was right and also what God said about adultery.

> Let marriage be honored among all and the marriage bed be kept undefiled, for God will judge the immoral and adulterers. (Heb. 13:4)

I deleted the message and resolved to not contact him in any way. When I felt tempted to do so in the weeks to come, I reached out to my close friends, and with their support and God's grace, I was able to avoid Satan's snare.

> Therefore, whoever thinks he is standing secure should take care not to fall. No trial has come to you but what is human. God is faithful and will not let you be tried beyond your strength; but with the trial he

will also provide a way out, so that you may be able
to bear it. (1 Cor. 10:12-13)

But just because Satan didn't trap me in adultery, that didn't
mean his attack on me was over. He would bombard me with negative thoughts about how unfair my situation was or entice me
down a trail of horrible "worst-case" scenarios in my mind about
how things would never get better. The more negative my
thoughts were, the more negative my words were. And even
though I thought venting about my situation would make me feel
better, it only made me feel more depressed and hopeless.

In addition to keeping my eyes fixed on Christ, my friend
Carrie also encouraged me to "speak life" over Tyler and my marriage.

Death and life are in the power of the tongue; those
who make it a friend shall eat its fruit. (Prov. 18:21)

But I hadn't yet learned that I could take my thoughts captive
and that I could choose to speak positively about my marriage
and husband, regardless of the circumstances. I felt that, if I did
so, I would be denying the situation and excusing Tyler from the
hurtful choices he had made. And in my opinion, he was to blame.

After months of wallowing in self-pity, I had lost my zest for
life, sense of purpose, and my usually positive outlook. I had gotten so used to tears and depression that it took looking at old photos one day to remind me of the woman I had once been. Back
then, I was confident and had a bright smile, a sparkle in my eyes,
and a peaceful countenance. But I was now just a shell of that
woman, and I didn't like who I had become. Regardless of what
happened with Tyler, I couldn't keep living like this. I pleaded for
God to rescue me from my pit of despair.

Graciously rescue me, God! Come quickly to help me,
Lord! (Psa. 70:2)

Personal Reflection & Group Discussion

How has or does Satan try to distract or tempt you?

What have you done or could you to do resist his attack?

39

SOMETHING HAS TO CHANGE

The next morning, I had just finished praying before work when something caught my eye. In a pile on my nightstand was the book, *Boundaries in Marriage*. I had purchased it months earlier but never even cracked it open. *Maybe it's time to actually read this*, I thought to myself as I picked it up and flipped through it.

A few hours later at work, my boss asked how things were going with me and Tyler. I told her that, some weeks, he would stop by, take me out, and be affectionate. The next week, I wouldn't hear from him. I didn't believe him when he told me he wasn't seeing other women, but because I wanted our marriage to work, I jumped at any chance to spend time together. It seemed like the right thing to do, but it was emotionally exhausting and confusing, and it made me feel like a doormat.

She listened sympathetically but then told me in no uncertain terms that allowing Tyler to have access to me whenever he wanted despite his unfaithfulness and abandonment was not helping. "Not only is it dishonoring and damaging to you, but if Tyler doesn't have to deal with the consequences of his behavior, he'll never change," she stated.

I had never thought of it that way. I assumed that, as a Christian wife, it was my duty to do whatever it took to save my marriage—even if it was hurting me. "What should I do?" I asked her.

"Establish healthy boundaries," she said.

That was the second reference to "boundaries" that day, and I sensed God was speaking to me. Just to make sure I got the message, he confirmed it through another coworker later in the day. She had been fasting all day, and in the middle of our conversation, she suddenly interrupted me. "Rachel, I don't know why, but I keep seeing this word 'boundaries' in my mind," she said. "Does that mean anything to you?"

I started reading *Boundaries in Marriage* as soon as I got home. Within a few pages, I felt like I had found a goldmine. The book gave practical advice about how to establish healthy boundaries that would not only prevent Tyler from unnecessarily hurting me but also create an environment where love could grow. I realized that my desire for a redeemed marriage was right, but my approach needed a lot of work. While I couldn't redo the past, I knew I needed time to process, pray, and seek God for guidance moving forward. I typed this email:

Tyler,

For months, I've tried to express to you how broken my heart is… how hurt I am and how empty and unloved I feel. Each time you call, text, or stop by to see me, I wonder, "Are his feelings changing?" Or I hang on your every word and silently pray that you will do or say anything to fill the aching emptiness in my heart that is so desperate for your love.

I'm 100% committed to this marriage. I have made many mistakes… and for those, I am truly sorry. I do love you, and I hope you never doubt that. But I realize there is nothing I can say or do to change you or cause you to love me. Only you can decide to take responsibility for your feelings, attitudes, behaviors, and choices. And the same goes for me.

I guess it never occurred to me that I have the freedom to respond, to make choices, and limit the ways your behavior affects me. I have felt like a victim of whatever you do or do not do. And that is not the truth. I am not a victim, but I also know that right now I don't know how to "walk that out." My eyes have been focused on you and not God, and I've been on an emotional roller coaster that has nearly destroyed me. I simply cannot live like this.

After praying, I know that I need some time apart from you. Please know that this is not me quitting on you or this relationship. I need time with the Lord so He can start healing me and reveal to me how to establish and live within healthy boundaries in this marriage.

Love,
Rachel

Personal Reflection & Group Discussion

What healthy boundaries do you sense God asking you to establish in your relationships?

How would living by those boundaries positively affect you? Your life? Your relationship? The other person?

40

THE TRUTH ABOUT TRAGEDIES

While we may not desire or be able to predict the tragedies or trials in our lives, we will face them nonetheless. Sometimes, bad things happen to good people. An illness strikes, a job is lost, a loved one dies, a heart is broken, or a marriage ends. Those experiences can be frightening, painful, and overwhelming, and they may even lead us to believe that things are hopeless.

The great news is that, no matter what your life looks like at this moment, there is hope. Jesus said,

> I have told you this so that you might have peace in me. In the world, you will have trouble, but take courage, I have conquered the world. (John 16:33)

Because of Christ's victory over death, we will ultimately have victory over every trial we face — if not in this life, absolutely in the next. Regardless of the challenges we face, we can take comfort in knowing that God will be with us every step of the way.

> Be brave and steadfast, have no fear or dread of them, for it is the Lord, your God, who marches with you; he will never fail you or forsake you. (Deut. 31:6)

I think of tragedies as the "storms" in our lives and God as the "sun." You may feel as though you've been under storm clouds and blocked from the sun's rays for as long as you can remember. You've learned to keep your head down to keep the rain out of your eyes. But in doing so, you missed seeing the times the clouds parted and the sun was shining directly on you.

Others of us have lived under "sunny" skies most of our lives. We know and have felt the blessing of God but not the pain of tragedy until, one day when the clouds rolled in, we found ourselves in the midst of a storm. We might have even wondered where the sun went and if God had abandoned us at the worst possible time. I assure you He didn't. God is no further away from us during the "bad" times of our lives than during the "good" times. It may look and feel that way, but unless we are the ones who moved, we can rest assured that God did not. And just behind those clouds, no matter how big and ominous they may seem, He is right there.

God is ready to take you by the hand and lead you through whatever you face in life, even the fiercest storm.

> For I am the Lord, your God, who grasp your right hand; It is I who say to you, "Fear not, I will help you." (Isa. 41:13)

It doesn't matter if you have made mistakes. We all have. It doesn't matter if you feel like your situation is impossible. Nothing is impossible for God. It doesn't matter if you don't believe God exists or that He loves you. This doesn't change the fact that both are true. And it doesn't matter if your life is an absolute disaster. God can redeem and restore anything.

Of course, I can't speak about your specific challenge or guarantee that all your problems and struggles will be resolved the way you want them to. In some cases, that happens. In others, it doesn't. But no matter what storm you are facing, I do know this: How we respond makes all the difference.

Anger, control, fear, abandonment, apathy, depression, and despair are the most natural human responses, and I've chosen all of them at some point. But no amount of anger caused the clouds to dissipate. Fear didn't calm the winds. None of my attempts at control made the storm go away. Not living my life didn't stop the rain from falling. And being depressed and giving into hopelessness not only made the storm seem worse than it really was, but it nearly destroyed me, too.

It wasn't until I was ready to hear and obey God that He began to show me there was a better way. And one by one, He revealed the five things I needed to do: let go, be open to change, walk by faith, forgive, and learn to love.

Personal Reflection or Group Discussion

How do you typically respond to the storms in your life? (Consider anger, control, fear, abandonment, apathy, depression, and despair.)

Have any of those responses positively changed you or your circumstances? If not, would you consider a different approach?

41

LETTING GO

The first thing God told me was to let go of trying to control and fix Tyler. Doing so wasn't effective and only led to stress, frustration, and exhaustion. But it wasn't easy because I still wanted my marriage to be redeemed. *Shouldn't I be doing something or saying something?* I'd think to myself. I can't tell you how many times I surrendered control to God only to snatch it back weeks, days, or sometimes even hours later. But besides my own sanity and quality of life, I needed to let go because, in the end, it would take both of us to make our marriage work. Even if I could convince Tyler to love me or force him to move home, it would be a temporary behavior change at best. And what I was praying for and knew only God was capable of causing was a heart change.

With God's help and a lot of will power, I stopped reaching out to Tyler, and he didn't reach out to me. For the first few days, it was hard, and the battle raged in my mind. *Is he still seeing this other woman? Why isn't he calling me? If I don't do something, will he think I'm giving up on our marriage? What will other people think?* But with each day, it got easier. When he was on my heart or mind, I'd pray and remind myself that God was in control. The more I turned to and surrendered my concerns to Him, the more peace I had and the more I realized that I still had a good life to live, regardless of Tyler and our broken marriage.

When I finally bumped into him a few weeks later, I knew in my heart he was still seeing this other woman. In the past, I would have asked questions or felt compelled to tell him how wrong his actions were, but I had learned the importance of setting boundaries and letting go. Tyler asked if I wanted to go to dinner, and rather than jumping at the chance, I took a moment to pray, and God gave me the words.

"Tyler, I told you that I would never divorce you, and I won't. You have the freedom to love me and the freedom to walk away, and there is nothing I can do about that. But I just want you to know that I've finally let go. I've let go of trying to control you... that's not by job. My job is to love you, and I'll continue to be faithful to my marriage vows and pray for you. But loving you doesn't mean I'm a doormat. I'm your wife, and I'm not willing to spend time with you as long as you're seeing this other woman. So, if you have ended things with her and you want to talk about healthy steps to move forward in our marriage, let me know. But if it's just taking me out to dinner to keep me on the back burner, I'm not interested."

Tyler was silent for a few seconds. He nodded soberly and said he understood. I had no idea what the future held for us, but I walked away with the peace and assurance that God was still in control and that I was doing exactly what He had asked me to do. *Let go.*

As I look back, I see that God has been asking me to let go for years. To let go of thinking my self-worth is based on my looks. To let go of striving for perfection or seeking the approval of others. To let go of expectations about what I think my life should look like. To let go of sin, unhealthy or toxic habits, and sometimes even relationships. And ultimately, to let go of regrets, insecurities, hurts, and anything else that God doesn't want me to hold onto.

While our human nature sometimes leads us to grasp and cling to things, God tells us to let go because carrying around a bunch of stuff drains us, robs us of peace, and steals our joy. He designed us to travel light on this journey called life, which means we have to make the daily decision to let go. That doesn't mean it's easy, you don't care, or you don't want the situation or person to be redeemed. It just means you accept that you can only control your own attitude and actions while the rest is in God's hands.

> Have no anxiety at all, but in everything, by prayer and petition, with thanksgiving, make your requests known to God. Then the peace of God that surpasses all understanding will guard your hearts and minds in Christ Jesus. (Phil. 4:6-7)

If you want to experience the peace that surpasses all understanding, surrender to God whatever He asks of you. Remember that He knows everything, He's in control, and He loves you and others more than you could ever imagine. So, let go, and let God be God.

Personal Reflection & Group Discussion

What is God asking you to let go of right now?

How would letting go positively impact your life and/or the lives of others?

42

BEING OPEN TO CHANGE

God made it clear that letting go was not about leaving Tyler or quitting on my marriage. I made a commitment to God and him through the good times and the bad, and that's what I was going to do. Yet, most of my prayers were pleading with God to convict Tyler of his sin. He was the one who was unfaithful and had moved out; therefore, he was the one who needed to change. Then, one day, I came across this convicting passage:

> Why do you notice the splinter in your brother's eye,
> but do not perceive the wooden beam in your own?
> (Matt. 7:3)

I had read that verse countless times, but I finally understood the second principle that God was trying to show me. Something absolutely needed to change… and it was me.

Attitude

For most of my life, I based my attitude on my circumstances and my emotions, both of which were generally very positive. When my marriage fell apart and I was discouraged and depressed, it occurred to me that I would continue to be so until my relationship was redeemed or my feelings changed… which I could not predict. Thankfully, God pointed me to something much more concrete and healthy to base my attitude on: His Word.

Reading the Bible daily reminded me that God chose me (Eph. 1:4-5). He reminded me that I am His priceless treasure, the one He died for (John 3:16), the one He loves unconditionally, and the one in whom He delights (1 John 3:1). He has a wonderful plan for my life (Jer. 29:11), nothing escapes His eye (Heb. 4:13), and He is working all things together for my good because I love Him and follow Him (Rom. 8:28). I will go through difficult trials, but Jesus overcame the sin of the world (John 16:33). I believe in Him. My true citizenship is in Heaven (Phil. 3:20), and He has reserved a place for me to spend eternity with Him there (John 14:1-3).

God's truth was a supernatural boost to me then and still is today. I can be confident and even optimistic in the midst of tough times because I know that every storm I face is temporary, God is with me, and He has a bigger purpose in mind—even if I don't see it at the time. Of course, there are days when I feel down, but when I look at myself and my situation in light of God's truth, focus on the positive, and remember what I have to look forward to in this life and the one to come, choosing a positive attitude becomes much easier.

Actions

Once my attitude changed, my actions naturally followed. Instead of feeling sorry for myself and looking for things to distract me from the storm I was facing, I started looking for healthy and positive ways to live through it. I might not have been able to change any of Tyler's actions, but I knew I could change mine. I recommitted to being the best version of myself spiritually, physically, emotionally, and relationally. I set goals and spent time cultivating my relationship with God, getting into great shape, reading books, and connecting with supportive friends and family members. Doing so gave me a renewed sense of purpose and helped me to become healthier and stronger in every area of my life.

Words

God also showed me I needed to change my words. Lamenting about my situation never truly made me feel better, so I made a concerted effort to live by this verse:

No foul language should come out of your mouths, but only such as is good for needed edification, that it may impart grace to those who hear. (Eph. 4:29)

I started taking Carrie's advice to "speak life" over every area of my life. It didn't matter what the facts were; I would look at the people and circumstances around me and describe them in light of God's truth. Instead of saying, "I don't know if my marriage is going to make it," I would say, "I believe one day I am going to have an amazing marriage." Or instead of, "It doesn't look like anything is changing," I would say, "I know God can do anything, and right now, He is working this out in my favor." Speaking life switched my focus from what was to what could be. And it turned my everyday words into powerful prayers and statements of belief.

Influences

What I listened to, read, and watched as well as who I associated with greatly influenced my life, and God began to show me that I needed to be discerning about all of those. The people who said things like, "I can't believe you're staying with Tyler after all of this," or "You deserve better than this," meant well; but they weren't helping. I needed people to pray with me, encourage me to continue being obedient to what God was asking of me, and remind me that I had what it took to endure this storm.

Besides surrounding myself with people like that, I found that being around alcohol and single men was often a source of temptation, so I made a concerted effort to avoid bars and similar environments. Certain television shows and movies put unrealistic expectations on what my life and marriage should look like, so I stopped watching them. And when I realized that looking at pictures and profiles of people in seemingly great marriages on Facebook didn't make me feel better about mine, I deactivated my account.

With more free time on my hands, I read books about struggling marital relationships and learned that many other people have faced incredible challenges and have chosen to fight for their marriages—even when it seemed hopeless. Their testimonies gave me the strength and courage to continue fighting for mine.

Expectations

Finally, God showed me I needed to change some of my expectations. I needed to stop expecting Him to solve all my problems when and how I wanted. I needed to stop expecting myself to have it all together and never make mistakes. And I needed to stop expecting to have a "normal and healthy" relationship with Tyler when he wasn't living at home. Those unrealistic expectations only added stress, frustration, and disappointment to my life. With God's help, I learned how to pray and hold high expectations for the future while living peacefully in the present, no matter what my circumstances looked like.

Changing your attitude, actions, words, influences, and expectations isn't something that happens overnight. True, lasting change takes time and effort. It requires us to do things differently, to be flexible, to grow, and above all else, to be open to the molding from God's hand.

> Yet, O Lord, you are our father; we are the clay and you the potter: we are all the work of your hands. (Isa. 64:7)

The good news is that, when you are open to change, you can trust that God will not only transform you in amazing ways but also into the incredible person He created you to be.

Personal Reflection & Group Discussion

In what area(s) of your life is God asking you to be open to change?

How would doing so positively impact your life or the lives of others?

43

WALKING BY FAITH

The third principle that God revealed to me was especially timely. After a year of separation and no change in our relationship, many people were encouraging me to move on or at least ask Tyler to file the paperwork to end our marriage. *Maybe they're right,* I'd think to myself. I knew divorce would be painful, but being single or starting over seemed better than being in limbo or trying to rebuild our relationship down the road. But time and time again, God would speak to me in that still, small voice and tell me to trust Him and walk by faith, to blindly follow Him down a road I had never been on, to listen and obey Him even when the voices around me told me otherwise, and to have faith that He was leading me exactly where He wanted me to go.

Of course, it was much easier to "walk by flesh," basing my decisions on my five senses or emotions. Doing so sometimes gave me temporary pleasure, but it was never truly satisfying in the long run and often hurt me or the situation. Other times, I got ahead of God, took the lead, and tried to figure things out on my own. And then, there were the times I simply sat down and refused to go where He was leading. Despite it all, God never gave up on me. He'd walk with me and tell me how much He loved me and that I could trust Him. He would remind me that, if I simply turned around and followed Him, He would guide me on the right path—even if I didn't know where it was leading. It reminded me of a prayer by Thomas Merton.

My Lord God, I have no idea where I am going. I do not see the road ahead of me. I cannot know for certain where it will end. Nor do I really know myself, and the fact that I think that I am following your will does not mean that I am actually doing so. But I believe that the desire to please you does in fact please you. And I hope I have that desire in all that I am doing. I hope that I will never do anything apart from that desire. And I know that if I do this you will lead me by the right road though I may know nothing about it. Therefore will I trust you always though I may seem to be lost and in the shadow of death. I will not fear, for you are ever with me, and you will never leave me to face my perils alone.

I didn't know where God was leading me or what was going to happen in my marriage, but He knew what obstacles were going to be in my path and what detours I would need to take to make it to my final destination. God never promised me that the road would be easy or that I wouldn't get a few bumps and bruises along the way. After all, living in a fallen world where people have free will makes that inevitable. He did promise me to be with me every step of the way, and I trusted that, wherever He was leading me, it was for my good.

I've learned that God is a highly creative communicator who is always speaking and that my job is to pay attention and listen. On a few occasions, I had a vision or sensed God speaking directly to me, but often, He spoke through the Bible. I found great peace in the unchanging direction and guidance it offered for every area of my life—my work, relationships, finances, health, and how to live abundantly with true peace and joy. Other times, God would speak to me through nature, music, and other people. Sometimes, it was an "ah ha moment," or something would just resonate deep within. Other times, it was when I was journaling or praying that

I got a clear sense of direction, felt convicted about something, or experienced a deep sense of peace.

However He chose to speak, as my relationship with God grew deeper, it became easier to recognize His voice.

> My sheep hear my voice; I know them and they follow me. (John 10:27)

I realized that He wanted me to walk by faith in every area of my life and at all times. Obedience is important in the "big" decisions but also in the seemingly small, daily ones. It doesn't always make sense, but if God is telling me to do or not do something, it's either to help me, help someone else, or prevent unnecessary hurt or pain. When I follow God implicitly, things inevitably turn out better than I could have imagined.

Despite what the world may say, following God doesn't mean you're weak or that you'll miss out on all the fun and pleasure in life. It takes an incredible amount of courage, strength, trust, and self-discipline to walk by faith. But when you do, you'll have the peace and joy of being in the center of God's will and having His supernatural protection and blessing.

> If you continue to heed the voice of the Lord, your God, and are careful to observe all his commandments which I enjoin on you today, the Lord, your God, will raise you high above all the nations of the earth. (Deut. 28:7)

Personal Reflection & Group Discussion

In what area(s) of your life is God asking you to walk by faith?

How would doing so positively impact your life or the lives of others?

44

FORGIVING

Tyler said he was sorry a few times. Being a good Christian, I told him I forgave him, but my forgiveness was conditional at best. I was still waiting for a truly remorseful and repentant apology and for him to move back home and work on our marriage. It wasn't until I was preparing for another hurricane that I realized a seed of bitterness had taken root in my heart.

As I secured the patio furniture and checked the windows, I thought back to the last hurricane when everything began to unravel. It had been more than a year, and I was still in a broken marriage, facing another storm, and was now alone. *Why isn't my husband here to help me?* I lamented angrily to God. *He's probably with this other woman. How can he be so selfish and uncaring!* I felt the resentment building within.

Tyler called and left a message a few hours later to see if I needed anything. This only further fueled my anger. *I don't want his help dealing with the hurricane. I want him to step up to the plate and deal with the storm in our marriage!* I stewed in my anger until my stomach was in knots and I had absolutely no peace. Then, I grabbed my journal and vented to God:

> Tyler offered to help with the hurricane preparations, but honestly, I don't want to give him the satisfaction of feeling like he's doing ANYTHING husband-like–because he's not. I'm not going to lie, God… today

was rough. I cried. I screamed and I ached with a broken heart. I know You are working this for my good, but it doesn't mean I enjoy this process. I don't know how to be myself around Tyler. He's hurt me so much I feel the need to show him my real emotions so he quits living in his selfish fantasy-land where he thinks nothing else matters but him and that his decisions don't hurt anybody else. They do. They hurt me! I know You have told me to wait, Lord. And out of obedience to You, I will. But I'm going to need Your grace every step of the way. Protect my heart, Lord. Please also protect me from this storm. I love you, Lord. I do have so much to be grateful for. Please help me remember that.

A few hours later, I got a short email from a missionary couple Tyler and I supported overseas. They were ministering to a family that was struggling with forgiveness and asked us to pray that they would reconcile with God and each other. They cited Matthew 18:21-22.

Then Peter approaching asked him, "Lord, if my brother sins against me, how often must I forgive him? As many as seven times?" Jesus answered, "I say to you, not seven times but seventy-seven times."

As soon as I read the verse, I felt conviction, but I didn't want to think about forgiveness—and certainly not toward Tyler. I pushed the feeling aside and headed to the gym to work out my frustration there. As I was driving, I turned on the radio, and the song "Forgiveness" by Matthew West came on. The lyrics talked about how forgiving is difficult and, sometimes, the last thing we want to do, but that only when we do so can we truly be free.

Hearing those words filled my eyes with tears. There was no doubt God was calling me to forgive Tyler, but just to make sure

I got the message, He spoke to me loud and clear later that night as I watched the movie, *October Baby*. Toward the end, there is a scene where a priest is talking to young woman in a church who is struggling with forgiveness. He quotes Saint Paul and encourages her with these words:

> Because we have been forgiven by God, we should forgive each other. In Christ, you are forgiven. And because you are forgiven, you have the power to forgive and to choose to forgive. Let it go. Hatred is a burden you no longer need to carry. Only in forgiveness can you be free. Forgiveness is well beyond your grasp or mine. Forgiveness you can't find on a trip or even in this cathedral. But if the Son shall set you free, you will be free indeed.

It was like God was talking directly to me, and I began to weep.

> I will give you a new heart and place a new spirit within you, taking from your bodies your stony hearts and giving you natural hearts. (Eze. 36:26)

The bitterness in my heart seemed to melt away as I remembered that God had, first and foremost, forgiven me for all my sins, the times I had disobeyed Him, and even the times I had hurt others. Humbled and grateful, I realized it wasn't a matter of whether Tyler deserved forgiveness. None of us deserve God's grace and mercy, yet He gives them to us freely. It wasn't a matter of whether Tyler had asked for forgiveness or was truly sorry. God was calling me forgive him anyway.

> Be kind to one another, compassionate, forgiving one another as God has forgiven you in Christ. (Eph. 4:32)

And it wasn't a matter of whether or not I had said, "I forgive you." True forgiveness was an act of the will, an intentional choice to let go of feelings of resentment toward Tyler.

That experience was the catalyst for me to truly forgive Tyler. This process took time, intentionality, humility, and relying on God's grace. I've learned that, even if the offense is significant, recent, happened long ago, or was perpetrated by someone who is no longer living, we can still forgive... and we should. Only when we let go of our hurt and resentment can we experience true serenity in our hearts, but the choice is up to us.

Recently, I saw someone on the news whose brother had been murdered. With seething anger, he claimed he would spend the rest of his life hunting down this killer so he would pay for his crime. While I can understand his pain and desire for justice, allowing his life to be consumed with hate and revenge won't bring his brother back. If anything, it will only destroy himself.

On the other hand, I know a woman who demonstrated Christ-like forgiveness to the man who brutally raped her. Despite the devastation and trauma he inflicted, she refused to harbor ill-will toward him and, instead, reached out to forgive him. Not only did this help her heal emotionally, but her act of compassion led to this man's repentance and conversion.

I've heard it said, "Forgiven, forgotten forever; that is what God can do." He does, and He will.

> As far as the east is from the west, so far have our sins been removed from us. (Psa. 103:12)

When we ask for forgiveness, God no longer remembers our sins, and we are seen as righteous in His eyes. It's not always as easy for us to see ourselves or others that way, but we should try. Even if we never forget the hurt we have endured or inflicted, God can still redeem it. I know that to be true in my own life, and it's helped me to find purpose in the pain and truly to forgive myself and others.

When I inevitably make mistakes and hurt others through my words or actions, I seek forgiveness from both God and that person as soon as possible. Most people are quick to accept an apology, but even if they aren't, I can be at peace knowing I've done my part to reconcile the relationship.

When I am the one feeling offended, I try to ask myself two questions. First, *Am I making this about me?* If so, I can stop right there and avoid wasting my time and emotional energy being offended.

Second, I ask, *Is this person intentionally trying to hurt me?* When I take the time to consider their motives, nine times out of ten, I am confident the answer is no. We are all imperfect people, and sometimes, we wound others without even realizing it.

Thinking about those two questions helps tremendously. When I do struggle with forgiveness, I remind myself that being offended and harboring resentment doesn't usually change the situation or person who has hurt me; it only steals my joy and makes me miserable. I have much better things to do with my time and energy than hold a grudge, and so do you.

If there is someone in your life you need to forgive or ask forgiveness from, I hope you will do so. This may not instantly erase or heal your past wounds or reconcile a relationship, but it is a major step in the right direction. And know that, when you choose to cultivate a heart of forgiveness, you choose to live free.

Personal Reflection & Group Discussion

Who in your life is God asking you to forgive or to ask for forgiveness from?

How would doing so positively impact your life and/or the lives of others?

45

LEARNING TO LOVE

Skydiving had always been on my bucket list, so when my friend suggested it, I seized the opportunity. I'd been up in a glider, ridden in the back of an F-15 fighter jet, and had never been fazed by heights. But it was totally different being 10,000 feet in the air, strapped to a man, and about to jump out of the side of a perfectly good airplane with nothing more than a piece of nylon attached to some strings to keep us alive.

After the initial shock of plummeting toward Earth in a free-fall, I looked at the world below me. Everything seemed so distant and small as did my own problems and worries. I was just one person in a world full of billions, each with their own litany of joys, pains, tragedies, and triumphs. Yet, I knew that my life mattered and that I didn't want to take it for granted. *What if my parachute malfunctioned and my life ended in 60 seconds? I could get cancer and be gone in 60 days or perhaps live another 60 years or more,* I thought.

I pulled the cord, and the parachute ripped open, yanking me up with such force that my legs flew straight out in front of me. It turned out I would have more than 60 seconds left to live. As I glided gently toward the ground, I vowed to make the most of whatever life I had left to live. I would live with the right perspective and focus: loving God, loving others, and loving myself.

Loving God

I decided to put forth the same effort in my spiritual health as I did my physical health. Like going to the gym, there were days I wasn't very motivated, but I knew that every moment I invested in my relationship with God was worth it. Reading the Bible, praying, journaling, and going to Mass gave me the wisdom, encouragement, peace, patience, and supernatural strength I needed.

One day, I felt particularly discouraged and went to church to pray. After about 10 minutes of venting all my fears, frustrations, unmet needs, and hurts to God, I sat in silence. It was comforting to know He was listening, He cared, and He could handle my raw emotion. *Is there anything You want to tell me?* I asked God. Deep inside I heard, *I am more than enough.*

God *is* more than enough—no matter what we are dealing with. There is no problem too big for God, no emptiness He can't fill, no need He can't provide for, and no heart He can't heal and cause to overflow with love. Knowing that, how could I not want to spend my life loving Him in return? Of course, my imperfect human love is nothing compared to His, but when I live my life to glorify Him and am grateful for every gift He has so graciously bestowed on me, it pleases Him and makes my life so much richer!

Loving Others

The more I focused on loving God and receiving His love, the better I was able to love others. The Bible says, "We love because he first loved us" (1 John 4.19).

Instead of seeing my marital struggle as embarrassing and something I needed to hide, I realized my experience and the lessons I'd learned could be valuable tools to help encourage others. Nobody seemed to think less of me because of my broken marriage. In fact, many thanked me for my transparency and found hope in my story. Maybe they couldn't relate to my exact situation, but nearly all could relate to facing a storm in life and needing to know how to get through it.

I felt led to lead a weekly women's Bible study in my home and asked God to help me minister to six other women. Each week, we learned together, shared our lives, and prayed for one another. Pouring into them took the focus off my own problems and helped me to find purpose in my pain.

> He who confers benefits will be amply enriched, and
> he who refreshes others will himself be refreshed.
> (Prov. 11:25)

Supporting each other through difficult times helped us to form strong bonds. We also made a point to celebrate the victories and good times, too. With a whole house to myself, I started cooking dinner for friends and hosting birthday parties and girls' nights.

One night, eight of us sat around my formal dining room table for a meal. I don't know how we got on the subject of embarrassing stories, but everybody started chiming in, and soon, we were laughing so hard we were all in tears. And that's when I noticed the sound. After Tyler moved his stuff out, I hated the empty echo sound in the house, but as the laughter bounced off the walls and filled every inch of my home, I thanked God for it and the joy and fullness that friendships brought to my life.

While it was easy to love my supportive family and friends, God was also calling me to love Tyler, too. Because he wasn't living at home, I didn't see him often, but whenever I did, I tried my hardest to live out 1 Corinthians 16:14: "Your every act should be done with love." I'd pay him a compliment or offer to help him out when he needed it. I'd remind him of his great qualities and pray for him. And even in the moments when I wanted to be rude or give him a piece of my mind, I'd ask God to help me be kind and loving. Or if that wasn't possible, I'd ask God to help me keep my mouth shut.

On more than one occasion, he looked at me with complete bewilderment. "I don't get it," he'd say. "After everything I've done, I don't understand how you are able to respond the way you are." I always told him what I knew to be true in my own heart: "It's just God working in me." Allowing Him to work in me to love Tyler and others brought newfound purpose and meaning to my life.

Loving Myself

Once I learned to love God and love others, it was much easier to love myself—not for what I looked like, how successful I was, what other people thought about me, or my relationship status... but for who He made me to be. Embracing my passions, I started taking a weekly Zumba class, tried new recipes, honed my cooking skills, and started drawing again. I read more books, watched great movies, went wine tasting, and realized I could have a great time with friends and also by myself.

In addition to taking up new hobbies and doing what I loved, God told me it was time to move forward with my dream of sharing the light of Christ with others by writing this book. In reflecting on my journey toward hope, I realized how far I had come. I no longer wanted to speed up time or wish away this season of my life. I wanted to live it fully and cherish every moment to love God, others, and myself and to squeeze every lesson I could from this experience.

The tragedy I once believed was the worst thing I could ever have gone through has ended up being the very best thing that has ever happened to me. I've never felt so whole, so free, or so confident. I've never laughed so much, been so grateful, or loved so well. And I've never been so full of hope, peace, and joy. While

I wouldn't have willingly chosen to endure this storm, I can honestly say I'm thankful for it because it's made me the woman I am today.

If you are facing a storm in your life, I hope you will let go, be open to change, walk by faith, forgive, and learn to love. Even if the sun is brightly shining and you can't see a cloud in the sky, I hope you will implement these five principles in your life anyway. Not only will you be prepared for any future storms, but it will make the great life you are living now even more amazing!

Personal Reflection & Group Discussion

How is God asking you to learn to love?

How would doing so positively impact your life and/or the lives of others?

46

PRACTICAL TIPS FOR MARRIAGE

I n the end, it takes two people to make any relationship work. With that said, regardless of whether you are living in wedded bliss, on the verge of a divorce, or hopeful that one day you'll find that special someone to share your life with, these three things will give you the best chance for success: 1) make God the center, 2) take 100-percent responsibility for yourself, and 3) expect tough times and refuse to quit.

1: Make God the center.

The best insurance policy for a marriage is making God the center of it. Not only does He want your marriage to flourish, but with Him at the center, you will have a supernaturally unifying force helping to strengthen your bond and protect your marriage against Satan's attacks.

A three-ply cord is not easily broken. (Ecc. 4:12)

Focusing on God also keeps things in perspective and reminds us that He is our eternal spouse and the only one who can completely fulfill us. The more we invite Christ into our heart and our relationship, the better able we will be to love our spouse the way God intended us to.

Wives be subordinate to your husbands, as is proper in the Lord. Husbands, love your wives, and avoid any bitterness toward them. (Col. 3:18-19)

You can do that by praying together, going to church, getting plugged into a Bible study, and earnestly trying to live out your calling as a godly husband or wife. Even if your spouse doesn't want to do those things with you, do them anyway, knowing that God will honor your efforts and will work in and through you to bless your marriage.

2: Take 100-percent responsibility for yourself.

While you can't control what your spouse will or won't do, you are responsible for your own attitude, actions, words, and the influences you allow in your life. Commit to doing your best in each of these areas, and when you mess up or miss the mark, own up to it. Apologize, learn from your mistakes, and move on. Refuse to blame your spouse, your job, or any other factor or situation for why you are short-tempered, selfish, or not fulfilling your role as a husband or wife.

Avoid the tendency to treat marriage like a contract. *If he does this, then I'll do that.* That sort of pettiness is divisive, and "keeping score" will only damage your marriage. In the end, it doesn't matter if your spouse lives up to his or her end of the marriage vows or not. You are accountable for how well you lived up to yours. So, make choices that honor God and your spouse and that you can be proud of.

3: Expect tough times and refuse to quit.

Every couple will experience difficult seasons in their marriage. Some may be relatively harmless and pass quickly while others might be devastating and may last for many months or years. Either way, I believe they should be endured. We live in a society that tells us marriage is disposable and that divorce is an option that many people resort to before they even try to work things out. When a couple is married,

> ...they are no longer two but one flesh. Therefore what God has joined together, no human being must separate. (Mark 10:8-9)

Marriage is a lifelong covenant that goes way beyond a wedding, a piece of paper, or tax benefits. It's worth fighting for even if it seems hopeless, you face betrayal, you believe you made a mistake by marrying this person, or you would rather be single or start over with someone else. Of course, situations of abuse are different, and if your relationship is unhealthy or putting you in physical or emotional danger, seek help immediately. Otherwise, make a commitment to love unconditionally, refuse to be moved by the storms that come, and resolve to be faithful no matter what. When you don't have any fight left in you, simply stand for your marriage, knowing that "The Lord himself will fight for you; you only have to keep still" (Exod. 14:14).

God promises that He will do His part if we will just do ours. This doesn't mean that marriage will be easy, you'll always feel in love with your spouse, or that there won't be temptations or days when you'll want to quit. It doesn't mean that your marriage will last a lifetime. I hope and pray it will. But even if it doesn't, you still have the opportunity to live up to your wedding vows every day and refuse to give up. So, be brave and steadfast, and give your marriage your all. It's worth it. You are worth it. And no matter what happens in the end, you'll be better because you fought for it.

Personal Reflection & Group Discussion

What are ways you can personally make God the center of your current or future relationship?

Who do you know who has demonstrated perseverance and steadfast commitment to their marriage vows, despite challenges? What can you learn from their example?

47

A DIFFERENT "WEDDED BLISS"

I used to think a great marriage was measured by how much passion and romance the couple had, how little they argued, how beautiful their home was, and how well-behaved their children were. While I'd like to have all those things one day, what truly defines a marriage is love—not the feeling but the verb. This kind of love puts another before oneself, requires sacrifice, and is what Jesus demonstrated when He chose to die on the cross.

Real love isn't motivated by feelings. I'm sure Jesus didn't feel like being crucified and having nails driven through His wrists and feet. But He was demonstrating and modeling what true, selfless love is… the willingness to lay down one's life for another.

> Greater love has no one than this: to lay down one's life for one's friends. (John 15:13)

We will not likely be asked to lay down our life for our husband or wife, but God does want us to learn to die to ourselves in small ways every day. Living up to our vows—to love and to serve, to be faithful and true, and to do so for better or worse and in sickness and in health—is not easy and requires discipline, selflessness, patience, and forgiveness. But in doing so, we are learning how to do the very thing we were created to do: love.

Years ago, I asked God to teach me how to really love. Now, I see that He has answered that prayer through my marriage to Tyler. I have learned how to love, and I've come to understand that it can take multiple forms. Sometimes, love is speaking a kind word, doing the dishes, or sharing an intimate moment. Other times, it is simply turning the other cheek and refusing to leave someone when that person is at his or her worst and is the most unlovable. And sometimes, love is just getting down on your knees and praying for that person when there is nothing else you can do.

It wasn't easy to love Tyler, but when I stopped looking for what I could get out of my marriage and started looking for what I could put into it, God led me to this verse:

> Likewise, you wives be subordinate to your husbands so that, even if some disobey the word, they may be won over without a word by their wives' conduct when they observe your reverent and chaste behavior. (1 Pet. 3:1-2)

My decision to be faithful and to love and respect Tyler not only honored him and God, but it allowed me to experience and understand what Jesus meant when He said,

> I have told you this so that my joy may be in you and your joy may be complete. This is my commandment: love one another as I love you. (John 15:11-12)

With that in mind, I have discovered "wedded bliss." It's not the bliss of a flawless husband or incredible marriage but the complete joy that comes from selflessly loving another. No matter what your marriage looks like, if you focus on doing the same, you can live in wedded bliss, too!

Personal Reflection & Group Discussion

How well do you truly love your spouse?

How would redefining wedded bliss as your ability to love your spouse selflessly change your outlook on marriage?

48

TANGIBLE TAKEAWAYS

Let Go

Let go of thinking it is your job to change your spouse.

If there is a serious issue you need to address, set aside time to communicate clearly, speak the truth in love, and set boundaries. But remember you are only responsible for your own actions and attitude—not the other person's.

Let go of comparing your spouse to anyone else.

Movies and television shows do not paint realistic pictures of marriage, nor does social media reveal what happens behind closed doors. When you are tempted to lust after someone else's seemingly perfect spouse, remind yourself that nobody is perfect, and thank God for the one you have.

Let go of any "affair" that dishonors God, your spouse, or your marriage.

It could be a person, pornography, romance novels, working overtime at your job, excessive time pursing a hobby, or excessive time with a group of friends. Ask God for help, and don't be afraid to reach out for support from a trusted friend, pastor, counselor, or coach.

Be Open to Change

Refuse to make hurtful jokes, criticize, or engage in "spouse bashing" with friends or family.

If you don't have anything nice to say, don't say anything at all.

Commit to reading a chapter each week from a book that expounds on marital relationships.

Consider *The Five Love Languages* by Gary Chapman or *Love and Respect* by Emerson Eggerichs.

Make a list in your journal of all the things you love about your spouse.

When you are frustrated or tempted to assume the worst about your spouse, refer back to this list and remind yourself of your spouse's great qualities.

Walk by Faith

Reflect on what God says about marriage:

> Love is patient, love is kind. It is not jealous, [love] is not pompous, it is not inflated, it is not rude, it does not seek its own interests, it is not quick-tempered, it does not brood over injury, it does not rejoice over wrongdoing but rejoices with the truth. It bears all things, believes all things, hopes all things, endures all things. Love never fails. (1 Cor. 4-8)

But from the beginning of creation, "God made them male and female. For this reason a man shall leave his father and mother [and be joined to his wife], and the two shall become one flesh." Therefore what God has joined together, no human being must separate. (Mark 10:6-9)

Wives be subordinate to your husbands, as is proper in the Lord. Husbands, love your wives, and avoid any bitterness toward them. (Col. 3:18-19)

Let marriage be honored among all and the marriage bed be kept undefiled, for God will judge the immoral and adulterers. (Heb. 13:4)

When one finds a worthy wife, her value is far beyond pearls. Her husband, entrusting his heart to her, has an unfailing prize. She brings him good, and not evil, all the days of her life. (Prov. 31:10-12)

Write a prayer in your journal asking God to help you more fully live out your calling as a husband or wife.

Or, re-write the following prayer:

Lord, thank You for the gift of my spouse. Please show me the big and small ways I need to die to self and put my spouse first. I know in loving my spouse I am loving You, so please help me do so in a way that honors You and makes my spouse feel loved and respected.

Stay committed to your calling as a husband or wife. If your marriage is healthy, consider encouraging and praying for couples who are struggling. If you are separated or going through a rocky time, consider going to counseling, ask God for help, and remain true to your marriage vows to every extent possible.

Forgive

Forgive yourself for the times you have not lived up to your marriage vows.

If you have hurt your spouse in any way, ask for forgiveness.

Forgive your spouse or ex-spouse for the times he or she has not lived up to his or her marriage vows.

Choose to forgive and let go of any bitterness you may be harboring in your heart.

Forgive others who have hurt you through their own inability to live up to their marriage vows.

It could be a parent, sibling, or children. If appropriate, consider writing a letter and giving it to that person, or keep it between you and God.

Learn to Love

Learn to love your spouse by setting aside time to talk openly about your relationship.

Ask questions and uncover how you can best express your love in a way that he or she prefers.

Learn to love your spouse by coming up with tangible daily, weekly, and monthly things you can do to better demonstrate your love and appreciation.

It could be writing a love note, taking out the trash, planning a date night, babysitting the kids, or giving your spouse some guilt-free time to hang out with friends, be alone, or pursue a hobby.

Learn to love God and your spouse by being complimentary and encouraging as often as possible.

Singing their praises will not only make your spouse feel valued, but you will be reminding both of you of his or her great qualities. People tend to live up to your words, so speak highly of them!

CHOOSING TO HOPE EVERY DAY

I finished the draft of this book the day before Easter. It seemed fitting, considering that no day represents more hope than the day we celebrate Jesus' resurrection and victory over death and sin. When I talked to my parents later that day, I told them, "I have never had a greater sense of expectation that my life is about to change dramatically." I couldn't explain how or what that would look like, but I sensed a shift was coming.

Three days later, Tyler showed up at my house. With tears in his eyes, he told me how sorry he was, that he was sure I was the woman God had for him, and that he was recommitting to me and our marriage. "I want to court you, and I am going to prove to you every day how much I love you," he told me. After nearly two years of unfaithfulness, I knew it would be a long road back to a loving, trusting relationship, but I was ready to try. So, we began dating.

A few weeks later, God confirmed something He had told me six months earlier during a day of prayer and fasting: it was time for me to leave Military Ministry. There was no explanation and no clear direction of what was to come. God just said, "The time is now."

My mind raced with practicalities. I hoped I could bargain with Him for more time and a few more paychecks to figure things out first. So, "now" is in a few months? I asked God.

Two weeks, I sensed Him say.

When I told Tyler, he was understandably a little concerned about making ends meet without my income. He asked what my job plans were, and I told him it had something to do with sharing this message of hope. He knew I heard from God clearly and also that I was going to obey Him.

"Okay, we'll make it work," he said.

I put in my two-week notice and began praying for clarity about life after Military Ministry. God inspired me with a business model and a name: "Choosing to Hope." With no entrepreneurial experience, I paid for coaching from experts who could help me position myself as an author, speaker, coach, and seminar leader. Given my passion, purpose, and natural gifts of speaking and encouraging others, it was the perfect fit, and I awoke each day eager to build my own business.

Just as I was getting settled in my new home office, the owner we had been renting from told us he wanted to sell the house. Tyler and I weren't looking to buy a home. We assumed we'd have some time to determine where I'd live or if we'd move in together somewhere. That all changed when, after a mere four days on the market, the house sold. I had a month till the new owners would move in.

I spent the next few weeks securing paper and boxes and packing up everything we owned. I didn't feel peace about moving into another apartment by myself or staying in Virginia. With all the memories and this other woman not far away, I wanted a fresh start. Texas was at the top of my list, and Tyler agreed to start looking for jobs there. We put everything we owned into two storage units, and to avoid getting locked into a lease, I moved into his apartment.

I knew our relationship was still not very stable, but I tried not to put any expectations on it or on Tyler. Instead, I focused on loving and respecting him to the best of my ability while working on my new business.

As the weeks went by, he still didn't have a job in Texas, and it didn't seem like finding one was a high priority. No matter what I did, Tyler wasn't happy, and he began to withdraw.

One night, I arrived home, and the house was empty. When I texted to see where he was, Tyler responded by telling me he was sorry and would always love me but that he wanted a divorce. He said he would be staying with someone else for the next several days to give me time alone and that we would talk soon. I didn't even know how to respond or what to say. I sat on the stairs in his apartment unsure of whether I was going to cry or throw up. *How could this have happened again? Where will I live? How will I support myself? How do I navigate a divorce?*

Like always, I called Carrie. Her words and prayers comforted me, but I couldn't sleep and spent most of the next day on my face crying out to God. It didn't make sense. Only a few months earlier, Tyler had looked me in the eyes and cried as he told me God had made it absolutely clear that I was the woman for him and that he would do whatever it took to make our marriage work. But here I was again. Rejected. Embarrassed. Confused. And all alone.

When I finally saw Tyler, he couldn't explain his change of heart, but he wasn't changing his mind. He had already met with lawyers and drafted a separation agreement. I was left with no choice but to move out. I was jobless, homeless, my marriage was ending, and almost everything I owned was packed up in a storage unit. I couldn't bring myself to move back home with my parents, nor could I afford my own place. Luckily, a good friend offered me a spare bedroom in her house for a few hundred bucks a month.

I arrived on her doorstep a few days later with all I had: a few suitcases of clothes, some food, a crushed spirit, and a broken heart. There were no tears left to cry. I just needed a roof over my head, peace, and time to heal. I figured I would start looking for a job, but God made it clear that accepting a position was not part of His plan for me. That was almost laughable. I was a perfectly capable adult with a master's degree and no income, and I wasn't supposed to work? "What am I going to be?" I asked God. "A stay-at-home woman with no house, husband, or kids?"

As I intentionally prayed, I realized that, though it seemed crazy, this was where the rubber met the road. Did I really believe everything I had just written about hope? Was I willing to let go, be open to change, walk by faith, forgive, and learn to love? If not, I had no business publishing this book or starting something called Choosing to Hope.

I pressed in to God as I worked on letting go of expectations, control, and concerns about what other people thought. I asked God to refine me even more as I prayed, fasted, and spent time reading the Bible. To the best of my ability, I obeyed His still small voice and walked by faith. Meanwhile, God was working in my heart, calling me to truly forgive Tyler and love those around me.

A few months later, I received my next instruction from God. *Start coaching.* It seemed a little crazy given my age and that I had no experience or formal training, but I took a step of faith and invested in an online coaching academy to hone my skills. The course gave me a coaching model and tips on how to market myself as a coach. A few weeks later, I was ready. I drafted an email to my entire contact list, offering each one of them a free 30-minute coaching session. I called it "Achieve your dreams in 2014" and hoped my rhyming name would be enough of a draw to generate some interest. It did, and I was thrilled to get my first client right before the end of the year. Everyone loved the free session and claimed they wanted me to coach them, but not everyone could afford it. A week later, I still had only one client, and I was getting worried.

That next Sunday at church, the pastor talked about Psalm 126:5: "Those who sow in tears will reap with cries of joy." He explained that the dreams of our hearts are the seeds that we sow and that we water them with our tears. I thought about my dream of God doing something big through me and my desire to share His light with others. *Yep, those dreams have definitely been watered with a lot of tears,* I thought to myself. But the pastor went on to say that there comes a time when we can actually over-water our field and drown our crops. "It's time to dry your eyes, get up, and expect to see fruit," he said. "Your harvest is coming."

That night, I went home and prayed to God. *Father, You know I didn't become a missionary because I care about money. But it would be nice to not have to live off my savings anymore.* I did the math and figured out what it would take to make ends meet. *I'm specifically asking for 10-15 coaching clients, God. You have always provided for me, and I trust that You will continue to.*

I continued my free coaching sessions, and miraculously, over the next 10 days, I got 10 additional coaching clients and more monthly income than I had asked for. How could a new business owner with no experience have clients and be profitable within two weeks? God.

I loved helping my clients get clarity about their goals and direction, strategize their actions, upgrade their skills, optimize their environment, and master their psychology. I also prayed for each one of them as I concluded our weekly calls. The weeks turned into months, and I began receiving emails, letters, and calls from clients expressing their gratitude and sharing their growth and success. I knew God and their own efforts were a big part of that, but I couldn't help but feel proud and that I was exactly where God wanted me.

Other than running into him once and the necessary emails and calls to sort out the divorce details, I didn't communicate or spend any time with Tyler. It was too painful. When he finally sent me the property settlement agreement, I looked it over and was about to sign it when I sensed God ask, *Did I tell you to sign that?*

I was confused. We had been legally separated for seven months, and I was ready to move on. *Maybe God just wants me to get legal counsel,* I thought. I made an appointment with a lawyer to go over the paperwork but felt sick to my stomach and unsettled during the entire meeting. That lack of peace was a clear indication I was outside of God's will, but I wasn't sure why. *Father, what do you want me to do?* I prayed. Instantly, I had a flashback of when Tyler had first come to me repentant and wanting to recommit to our marriage. The last thing he had said to me was, "Thanks for not quitting on me." I remembered the tears in his eyes and the look on his face, and I immediately sensed what God was saying to me. *You're not to quit on him.*

I wasn't sure what I would say to family and friends who were all expecting the divorce to be finalized soon, but the first person I needed to talk to was Tyler. He agreed to meet me for coffee, and I shared with him what God had told me. "After a full year of separation, you can file the paperwork and divorce me without my signature," I said. "But I simply can't sign this paperwork." Tyler said nothing for several minutes. When he finally spoke, he admitted that he still had feelings for me. He was hesitant to say much, but he reiterated that he loved me and would be praying. "I guess we have another five months to figure it out," he said.

I had been living in Hampton, Virginia with my friend the whole time, but her roommate would soon be returning from a deployment, so it was time for me to find a new place to live. While my business was doing well, I wasn't making enough to afford a place of my own—at least, a decent one in a safe part of town. I didn't know where I was going to go, but I sensed God saying once again, *Just trust me.*

A few days later, I drove to Virginia Beach to have lunch with a new friend. I had met Jill and her family at a prayer meeting a month earlier, and we had an instant connection. She invited me to her gorgeous home on the river, and we enjoyed the view as I updated her about Tyler and the fact that I was looking for a new place to live. Her husband came home for lunch, and both of them prayed for me and that God's hand would direct and guide my next steps.

I left feeling refreshed by the conversation, company, and the surroundings. There was something about being on the water that was so healing to my soul. *Wouldn't it be amazing to live at a place like that?* I thought to myself. About 45 minutes later, I had just arrived back home when my phone started ringing. It was Jill. "Are you ready for this?" She proceeded to tell me that her husband had made an unbelievable proposal; they would fix up their mother-in-law suite so I could live there.

I was blown away by their offer, especially because we had only met a few times. Jill reassured me that her husband did not make rash decisions and that God had clearly told him to do this. It was hard to argue with that, but I was still hesitant. Was He really calling me to move in with this family? To be 45 minutes away from all my friends?

Because the space needed some major work, Jill said it would take at least a month to get it ready. They were meeting with the contractors the next day, and she would keep me posted. I promised to pray about her offer and hung up the phone as I tried to take it all in.

The next morning, I woke up early to pray before I headed over to meet Carrie. She was always my sounding board and prayer support when I faced big decisions, and I wanted her perspective on all of this. *God, if you really want me to move down to Virginia Beach, I want confirmation today while I'm with Carrie*, I prayed. Considering that I needed to be out of my place as soon as possible, I added another condition. *And it will have to be ready in two weeks.*

I spent the morning with Carrie and filled her in on everything. Just when we were about to eat lunch, Jill called. She said they met with the contractors that morning and were beginning work that very day. Because I hadn't seen it, she told me that it had a full kitchen, living room, bedroom, and bath. It had a dishwasher, washer and dryer, two outside doors, and its own parking space. If I moved in, there would be no lease, and I could come and go as I wanted. I'd have access to their saltwater pool, hot tub, dock, and kayaks whenever I wanted. "Whatever you can afford to pay us for rent is fine," she said. "And by the way, it'll be ready in two weeks."

My mouth fell open, and I couldn't speak. When I finally did, I couldn't control the emotion. "I'm so overwhelmed at the goodness of God," I cried. There was no way I could have ever afforded to live in a place like that, not to mention with such an incredibly godly family.

I told my friends and family, and they, too, were amazed at how God was providing for me. After a few weeks and several trips to the storage unit, I was happily settled into my new place in Virginia Beach. Tyler wanted to see it and offered to drive down and bring a few things to me that I had forgotten. It was our first time really hanging out in nine months, and I didn't know what to expect. Before he arrived, I got on my knees and prayed for God to bless our time together. Things went better than I could have expected. We enjoyed each other's company, and while we didn't discuss the future, there was undeniable chemistry between us.

This was the first of several dates we would have over the summer. With his travel schedule and the distance between us, I only saw Tyler a few times a month. He never wore his wedding ring or talked about any kind of commitment to me or our marriage, and by the end of the summer, I was getting anxious. It was about to be the three-year mark of when everything had first fallen apart and the one-year mark of our separation. At that point, Tyler would be free to file the divorce paperwork.

I didn't know what was going to happen, but when a close mutual friend told me that Tyler never mentioned me and that he was seeing other women, my heart sank. Nothing had changed. I wanted to call and tell him to proceed immediately with the divorce paperwork, but I'd learned that reacting in anger never ends well. I went to church to pray instead.

While at church, God reminded me of the book of *Hosea* in the Bible, a book that several other people had encouraged me to read over the last few years. The first three chapters tell the story of the prophet Hosea who was married to Gomer, a faithless prostitute who left him again and again. Despite his pain and embarrassment, God repeatedly told Hosea to take her back which he did because, in doing so, he was modeling God's approach toward us: He loves us unconditionally and will always welcome us home, no matter how many times we stray.

Like Hosea, God was calling me to preach that same message through my marriage to Tyler. After a few days to pray and get my heart right, I met with him. "Tyler, I love you, and I have forgiven you," I told him. "There is an open door to my house and my heart... all you have to do is come home."

Though he never directly responded to that statement, I knew I had done all I could. The decision was completely up to him. Weeks went by, and though I didn't see or hear from him, I continued to pray and surrender Tyler and my marriage to God.

One morning at daily Mass, the priest talked about how Mary, the mother of Jesus, perfectly modeled how to suffer with grace, humility, and perseverance. As I reflected on her example, I earnestly prayed for the ability to do the same. *Lord, if Tyler never comes home... if he's never faithful... if we never have a family... I accept. I will love him all the days of my life and be joyful and thankful... even if things never change.*

Supernatural peace filled my heart. I went up for communion, and when the minister offered me the chalice, I heard the audible voice of God for the second time in my life. "Can you drink the cup that I drink?" Once again, I glanced around on the off chance it was another person speaking, but I knew deep down it was a message just for me.

The "cup" referenced Jesus' suffering and death on the cross. While I was sure I could not endure that, I was confused. Only five minutes prior, I had finally accepted the suffering of my marriage with joy and peace. *What are you trying to tell me?* I prayed as I knelt in the pew. I closed my eyes and saw a vision of the sun setting. Though I didn't hear any clear message from God, I got the distinct feeling that something was about to change.

I awoke the next morning with unbelievable peace and joy. *Where is this coming from?* I wondered. Immediately, I remembered the vivid dream I had. In it, Tyler and I got divorced, and there was nothing but serenity, love, and respect between us. I gasped. *Was God really releasing me from my marriage?*

I asked God to speak to me, and that's when I heard in my spirit, *I do not allow my children to suffer one minute more than is necessary. It is finished.*

Tears filled my eyes, and goosebumps covered my body. I had waited years, hoping and praying for redemption, and that's when it occurred to me. It had been three years exactly since I first found out Tyler was having an affair. After giving him every opportunity to repent and recommit to our marriage, it seemed God was finally releasing me so I could move on.

This was not what I was expecting. Only a few days earlier, I had peacefully resigned to remain married to Tyler even if things never changed. To be sure I was hearing from God and not some other voice, I made plans to meet with Carrie the next day and asked Jill and her husband if I could talk with them that night.

After telling them everything, they agreed that God had clearly spoken to me. "When are you going to tell Tyler?" they asked. We hadn't seen each other in almost a month, and I figured I would wait until he reached out to me. No more than two minutes later, Tyler texted me. I told him we needed to talk, and we made plans to meet the following afternoon after my visit with Carrie.

Jill and her husband prayed over me, and I returned to my apartment. I, too, believed I was in the center of God's will, but just to be sure, I grabbed my Bible. *Lord, this whole time, You have told me not to quit. So, if You are really releasing me from this marriage, please confirm it through Your Word.*

I randomly opened my Bible like I had done countless times over the years when I needed a clear word of encouragement from

God. Repeatedly, it had opened to Jeremiah 32 where I had verses 17 and 27 underlined. Both stated that God was the God of the impossible and that there was nothing He couldn't do. Those verses had given me the strength and courage to not quit on my marriage when I was most discouraged. But this time, the Bible didn't open to Jeremiah 32. It opened to the page before, something that had never happened.

What's in Jeremiah 31? I wondered. And that's when my eyes focused on the heading of the paragraph I was looked at. In big bold letters, it read, "End of Rachel's Mourning." I blinked in disbelief. In the paragraph below, there were several verses that I had previously underlined but hadn't seen in years.

> Thus says the Lord: Cease your cries of mourning, wipe the tears from your eyes. The sorrow you have shown shall have its reward, says the Lord... There is hope for your future, says the Lord... (Jer. 31:16-17)

Not only did God speak directly to my situation and give to me hope about the future, but he actually used my name. There was no possible way for God to be clearer than that. "Thank you, Lord," I said. It was the confirmation I needed, and I went to sleep hopeful that my season of mourning was finally coming to a close.

When I met with Carrie the following day, she too sensed God had spoken to me clearly. We reflected on the ups and downs of the three-year journey that had brought us so close together. It was not the ending either of us expected or wanted, but knowing I had done everything possible to love Tyler and fight for our marriage, I had no regrets. "I have watched you transform beautifully through all of this, and I'm so proud of you, Rachel," she said.

"I couldn't have done this without you," I choked. We both cried as we held hands and prayed for my conversation with Tyler.

When we met, I shared with him everything God had spoken to me. "Tyler, I married you because God told me to. I have stayed with you this whole time because God told me to. And now, God has released me from this marriage, and I'm asking you to release me, too." My heart pounded as Tyler sat in silence, processing those words. I could see the emotion on his face. Finally, he spoke. "Yes." He wiped his eyes and swallowed hard. "You deserve better."

We talked for the next hour about everything. He told me that he was so sorry, regretted hurting me, and wished he could go back and do things differently. "I love you, Rachel," he said with tears in his eyes. "I always will." I put on a brave face when we hugged goodbye, but it still felt as though my heart was ripped apart. I would always love him, too.

When I got back to my place, I knew what I needed to do. On my left hand was the beautiful engagement ring I had worn faithfully for more than five years. It was engraved with the word "Streetlights", a reminder of the sign God had given to us that we were supposed to be together. My wedding band was engraved with "God's timing is always perfect." In the years of separation, those rings had often been the most tangible part of our marriage, and I had never taken them off.

As I slid the rings off my finger, I wept uncontrollably. Though God told me that it was the "End of Rachel's Mourning," I knew it would take time and also that I needed to grieve the death of our marriage and all the dreams I had for it. While the divorce was heartbreaking and something I never expected to go through, it was an instrumental part of my journey to hope.

I know you won't remember all the details of my story, but I wanted to give you tangible examples of what choosing to hope looks like every day. It doesn't always make sense. It isn't always what you want to do. And sometimes, it feels like the hardest thing you've ever had to do. But I can promise you this: choosing to let go, be open to change, walk by faith, forgive, and learn to love is the best thing you will ever do.

Not everyone is called to share their story publicly like this. But I believe God has asked me to do so because stories like these need to be told. We need people to be authentic and allow God to use their pain and experiences in life to minister to others. We need people who can look us in the eye and admit, "I've been where you've been." And also, "With God's help, you're going to get through this."

I'll admit that it was a little scary at first. I wasn't sure if people would judge me or think less of me for being transparent about everything that has happened in my life. Then, I remembered that I'm not looking to win the approval of others. I'm looking to win hearts for Christ. With that in mind, I wrote this poem to share on Facebook to encourage others. I hope it inspires you.

> I'm not one to post a lot of personal stuff online.
>> After all, aren't we all supposed to pretend everything's just fine?
>
> So, I debated and waited and took some time to pray
>> and sort of hoped this conviction to share would go away.
>
> But it didn't, and so here, vulnerably I am,
>> not looking for sympathy or trying to win fans.
>
> Just wanting to be authentic as I share from the heart
>> that, unfortunately, my marriage has fallen apart.
>
> I never would have guessed I'd be divorced one day.
>> I thought we'd be together forever growing old and gray.
>
> The details of our relationship aren't part of this post
>> because, in the end, that's not what matters the most.
>
> The truth was that, initially, I felt nervous and ashamed
>> to go on Facebook and change back my name.

I feared what all these people would think and say,
   not that my personal life is the focus of your day.

Would people think I quit or didn't fight with all I
   had?
   Or that I just casually got divorced, and it didn't
   make me sad?

Neither is true I just want to confess
   the last several years have been quite a painful
   test.

Perhaps you understand and can possibly relate.
   After all, no one's life is perfect even if their profile looks great!

The storms of life we will face are sure indeed,
   but I've learned that how I respond is entirely up
   to me.

Through the hardest season I've experienced in life,
   I've grown stronger and discovered hope in the
   midst of strife.

Now, I won't despair when the storm winds start to
   blow.
   I'll just ask God to hold my hand and help me to
   grow.

Because in every trial, there's a lesson to learn,
   and if we do, it makes our trust in God that much
   more firm.

So, I'll face future storms with confidence and faith,
   knowing that, with God on my side, I have what
   it takes.

In the end, enduring this trial has awakened a deep
   desire,

a dream and passion burning with unquenchable
fire.

To be my best self and help others do the same
is better than all the world's money, riches, or
fame.

So, for that, I'm so thankful as well as for great family and friends.
They've been with me faithfully through thick
and though thin.

To everyone who's married, my prayers and best
wishes for you.
No marriage is easy—I know you know that's
true!

And for those of you separated or in a tough place,
I hope you fight for your marriage and rely on
God's grace.

For those who did all they could and their marriage
didn't last,
I'm so sorry and hope you're able to let go of the
past.

No matter where you are in life, I'm sure that you
know
your attitude and actions determine where you
will go.

It's true things didn't turn out the way that I hoped,
but I'm far too blessed to sit around and mope.

So, I'll keep choosing to hope, love well, and even
have some fun
because, thanks to God, I truly believe the best is
yet to come!

Personal Reflection & Group Discussion

In what area of your life is God asking you to choose hope today?

How can you learn from or encourage others with storms you have faced in the past or are currently facing?

FINDING TRUE HOPE

I used to think that, to live the "fairytale," my life needed to follow a pretty standard plotline and include five essential elements. But while there is nothing wrong with wanting beauty, success, significance, an incredible romance, and wedded bliss, I've come to understand that God doesn't define those the way most of the world does.

In God's eyes, beauty is about more than what you look like on the outside; it's about who you are on the inside. Success is more than your job title or paycheck; it's following your God-given passions and pursuing your dreams. Significance is more than others' opinions of you; it's knowing your inherent self-worth, becoming fully who God made you to be and doing what you can to serve others. An incredible romance is more than being swept off your feet by another person; it's embracing the undying, passionate, and eternal love God has for you. And wedded bliss is more than being in a seemingly perfect marriage with no problems; it's learning how to love another selflessly.

With this new perspective, my idea of a fairytale life already looks completely different. And God isn't simply limited to just a few plotlines. No matter where we have been, where we are now, or where we'd like to end up, if we follow God, He will use everything in our life and work it all together for our good—even the tragedies.

We know that all things work for good for those who
love God, who are called according to his purpose.
(Rom. 8:28)

With God, there are infinite possibilities, but there is still one
variable: *you*! You choose your attitude and actions, so decide
right now to let go, be open to change, walk by faith, forgive, and
learn to love. If you've made it this far, I hope you've worked
through the "Tangible Takeaways" at the end of each section already. If you skipped over them, go back now and do them. I truly
believe, if you will apply them, not only will you rediscover hope
but you will learn the best response to the inevitable storms of life,
choosing to dance in the midst of them.

That's exactly what I'm doing. I'm choosing to lift my arms
up and twirl around as the rain comes down. I'm choosing to
laugh loudly and dance around as the wind plays with my hair,
sending it in a thousand different directions. I'm choosing to live
freely, completely authentic and comfortable in my own skin with
a zeal for life that isn't dependent on my circumstances or other
people's opinions of me. I'm choosing to cultivate my internal
beauty, pursue my God-given dreams with passion and purpose,
be fully myself, serve others, and love with every ounce of my
being. No storm is going to keep me from living an amazing life,
and I no longer feel pressured to try to have a perfect one. After
all, I have the perfect God, and He's given to me true, unbounded
hope.

I have hope that, one day, I will marry an amazing man and
God will redeem my broken marriage. I have hope in knowing
that, no matter what, I am better because of what I've experienced
and that God has redeemed me. I have hope in knowing that
storms will come and go, but I still get to choose my response to
them. And I have hope in knowing that, regardless of what may
happen in this life, I have a bright and wonderful future ahead
because, with Christ, I have a fairytale with a guaranteed happy
ending—eternity with Him. And that's the best hope there is!

Therefore, since we have been justified by faith, we have peace with God through our Lord, Jesus Christ, through whom we have gained access by faith to this grace in which we stand, and we boast in HOPE of the glory of God. Not only that, but we even boast of our afflictions, knowing that affliction produces endurance, and endurance, proven character, and proven character, HOPE, and HOPE does not disappoint, because the love of God has been poured out into our hearts through the Holy Spirit that has been given to us.

—ROMANS 5:1-5

EPILOGUE

My hope journey continues, and I'm truly grateful for where God has led me spiritually, relationally, and physically—including a year-long trip where I circumnavigated the globe. Perhaps my second book will highlight that adventure!

From the bottom of my heart, thank you for taking the time to read and share in my story! If it has challenged, encouraged, or inspired you, please take a few minutes to share your thoughts or simply let me know how I can pray for you. You can contact me via www.RachelSherburne.com. I would love to stay in touch!

May God bless you and fill you with unbounded hope,
Rachel